Soldiers of Von Thoma

Soldiers of Von Thoma

Legion Condor Ground Forces
in the Spanish Civil War

Lucas Molina Franco
& José Mª Manrique Garcia

Schiffer Military History
Atglen, PA

"...In the history of modern warfare, [the *Legión Cóndor*] was absolutely unique, not only as regards its structure and use, but in its merits as well. Each member was selected within his speciality, whether it was an airman or a tank crew, a radio operator or a gunner, a car driver or a seaman, a technician or a translator, and according to his specialized intellectual capacity, thus making up an elite group in the best sense of the word..."

Wilfred von Oven
(*Hitler y la Guerra Civil Española.*
Misión y destino de la Legión Cóndor)

Book translation by Juan Carlos Salgado Rodriguez

Book Design by Ian Robertson.

Copyright © 2008 by Lucas Molina Franco & José Mª Manrique Garcia.
Library of Congress Control Number: 2008921641

Printed in China.
ISBN: 978-0-7643-2926-5

This book was originally published in Spanish under the title
Los hombres de von Thoma by Quidrón Ediciones

We are interested in hearing from authors with book ideas on related topics.

Published by Schiffer Publishing Ltd.
4880 Lower Valley Road
Atglen, PA 19310
Phone: (610) 593-1777
FAX: (610) 593-2002
E-mail: Info@schifferbooks.com.
Visit our web site at: www.schifferbooks.com
Please write for a free catalog.
This book may be purchased from the publisher.
Please include $3.95 postage.
Try your bookstore first.

In Europe, Schiffer books are distributed by:
Bushwood Books
6 Marksbury Avenue
Kew Gardens
Surrey TW9 4JF, England
Phone: 44 (0) 20 8392-8585
FAX: 44 (0) 20 8392-9876
E-mail: Info@bushwoodbooks.co.uk.
Visit our website at: www.bushwoodbooks.co.uk
Free postage in the UK. Europe: air mail at cost.
Try your bookstore first.

Contents

Foreword

The emergence of new historical document sources has always been a reason for satisfaction to all those interested in the subject, and particularly for those who have studied and researched it.

The pleasure is even greater when the matter has been treated, for decades, with lack of accuracy and even little respect for the facts, as is the case with the German tanks and the anti-tank guns in the Spanish Civil War.

It was von Thoma himself who contributed to the confusion created about these subjects with his statements to Captain Liddell Hart, in which he maintained that he had commanded four tank battalions (twelve companies) and thirty anti-tank gun batteries in Spain, or at least that is what the versatile British Captain understood and Hugh Thomas popularized. Intrigued with that statement, which became the basis for all sorts of exaggerations, I studied the subject forty years ago and came to the conclusion that the number of tanks supplied by Germany could not have exceeded one hundred and forty-eight. My statement drew harsh criticism.

This matter has now been totally clarified thanks to the new information recently arrived at the *Archivo General Militar* in Ávila from the *Jefatura de Movilización, Instrucción y Recuperación* (M.I.R.),[1] a body that operated very efficiently from 1937 to the immediate post-war, which has been studied in detail by Lucas Molina and José María Manrique and has led them to the conclusion that the tanks actually supplied to the Nationalist Army numbered one hundred and twenty-two. In their previous book, *Legión Cóndor. La Historia olvidada*, they had explained that those included in the accounts of the *Legión Cóndor* were seventy-two, to which they have added now the fifty acquired through HISMA.

Molina and Manrique explain that the first seventy-two tanks were allotted to the so-called *Gruppe Drohne*, the largest contingent of which arrived in Seville by ship on 8 October 1936, before the establishment of the *Legión Cóndor*, and was used to establish a battalion with two tank companies (sixteen tanks each and nine reserves) and Transport, Workshop, and Anti-tank Training (twenty-four 37-mm guns) companies. The authors then add that a few days later von Thoma assumed command of the battalion, and that a further twenty-one tanks and thirty-seven men arrived in Seville on 25 November; both were used to establish the third tank company of the battalion, which had up to sixty-two tanks and three hundred and seven men by late 1936, a figure that was reduced to one hundred and twenty-four by 1937, and later to one hundred and eight. In 1937 the tanks increased with a further ten early in the year and thirty in August, and men were reduced to one hundred and twenty-four, as the number of Spaniards trained grew. The last twenty tanks arrived in 1939.

The authors explain that, by the end of the war, there were eighty-four German tanks on the inventory (manned by Spaniards)—only thirty-eight less than those received, which proves the great efficiency of the repair workshops, as the figures of tanks temporarily out of service were much larger than the total losses.

Molina and Manrique devote the first half of their book to show carefully the operation of *Gruppe Drohne*. The alphabetic name lists compiled by the authors show the four hundred members who served in the group during the war, with ranks and induction and discharge dates in the group (either by new postings, repatriation, or death), and are indisputable evidence of the reliability of their information sources and the attention paid to detail in their work.

From the data supplied by the authors on the tank crews killed in action—six in total— one comes to the conclusion that the battalion was basically employed in training and logistic missions, and the crews rarely took part in war operations. As regards anti-tank gun batteries, the book confirms that the personnel were Spanish, except for the ones in the first battery, although they were trained by the personnel under von Thoma's orders. The fact that the latter was appointed Inspector of all tank forces (German, Italian, and Spanish) and anti-tank batteries explains his statement to Liddell Hart.

As regards the second main subject in the book, the German contribution to the training in the Infantry officer and NCO courses, it is the first time that it gets an in-depth treatment. Gárate's classic book on the training of *alféreces provisionales* (temporary second lieutenants) certainly mentions the German instructors and their early work at the Falangist *Academias de Mandos*, but does not include data regarding the numbers of those instructors, their distribution by school, and the time they stayed in Spain, which is dealt with in detail in *Von Thoma's Men*. The instructors who came from Germany in February 1937 for that purpose were later joined by many of those who initially served in *Gruppe Drohne* and by some who arrived later, as is explained by the authors.

The absence of previous studies on the third main subject of the book, the German training in the Artillery, mine throwers, Engineers (Signals, Sappers, and Chemical Warfare), and the *Escuela Naval*—Naval School— courses, is even more conspicuous, for which reason the information supplied by Molina and Manrique fills in the information gap existing so far. It is interesting to remark that, since the German air aid was the most important, it was precisely the flying schools that did not have German instructors.

This book *Von Thoma's Men* goes beyond the title, as it also deals with another matter, which comes as the fourth great subject—although in less detail—the Staff of Lieutenant Colonel von Funck, von Thoma's hierarchic superior in Spain, and the Radio Monitoring Group.

The undoubted interest of the text is supplemented by a large photo selection that increases, even more, the value of the work.

Madrid, 6 November 2003
Jesús Salas Larrazábal

Introduction

There is no doubt that one of the most important subjects, both for researchers and aficionados, in the historic context of the Spanish Civil War has been—and will probably remain—the study of foreign participation in the Spanish conflict. And it is obvious that most of the interest has been drawn to this day—although it is not the only one—by the German contingent known as the "*Legión Cóndor*."

Numerous Spanish and foreign works, some of them better, some worse, have dealt with the participation of the German air units in the Spanish Civil War to the last detail. And, although all those works refer to the presence in Spain of a contingent of the German Army (*Heer*), none of them has included an in-depth study, independent of the larger unit it was part of.

This land contingent, whose codename was *Imker* (beekeper), was organized by *Oberstleutnant* Walter Warlimont, the liaison officer between the *Heer* and the *Cuartel General del Generalísimo*—the Generalissimo's HQs, C.G.G. for short—although, from November 1936 it came under the auspices of the officer of the same rank, Hans *Freiherr* von Funck, who was the German Military Attaché in the Nationalist area for the duration of the whole war.

Gruppe Imker was made up of a Staff group (*Imker Stab*), an armored group (*Imker Panzer Gruppe Drohne*, also called *Gruppe Thoma*), and a radio monitoring company (*Imker Horch Kompanie*, also known as *Gruppe Wolm*), as well as the relevant services to carry out their tasks at Franco's HQs (including *Imker Ic.*, i.e. the Intelligence Section). These units, unlike those dispatched by the *Luftwaffe*—the backbone of the *Legión Cóndor*—could not be regarded as fighting forces at all, no matter what the widely published sources on the German unit may have said. They were, in all cases, basic and specialized training units (in the case of *Gruppe Thoma*) or intelligence interception and processing units, as in the case of *Gruppe Wolm*. The death in action of some of its members denotes the involvement and the effort made by the German volunteers in their training tasks of the Spanish soldiers in the use of German equipment.

In January 1937, several German officers of the *Heer*, under *Oberstlt* Walter von Issendorff's orders, arrived in Spain with the specific task to give military training to the officers of the *Falange Española de las JONS* Militia.

These Germans thus became part of the teaching staff of the Falangist officer academies in different Spanish towns, although the best known was certainly that at Pedro Llen, Salamanca, directly involved in the events that led to the Unification Decree, the closure of all the Falangist training schools and the incarceration of many members of the *Falange*—including their national leader, Manuel Hedilla Larrey. By early May 1937, once the conflict was solved, this group—which was known as *Gruppe Issendorff*, after the name of their first chief—came under the authority of *Ritter* von Thoma, and now served at the Infantry academies for temporary second lieutenants and sergeants, a mission that the *Imker* had just assumed. Its official name was *Imker Ausbilder*, i.e. Instructors of the group of the German Army operating in Spain.

As the Italians also became involved in the training tasks of the temporary officers and NCOs, and clearly in order to avoid brushes between Latins and Germans as far as possible, the Spanish high command decided that the III Reich instructors should operate at all the Infantry academies, and the Italian military in the rest. Despite this delineation of the respective fields of action, *Imker Ausbilder*—on the initiative of their chief, Colonel von Thoma—organized small Artillery and Engineers instructor units (*Gruppe Lutz* and *Gruppe Siber*), and even collaborated with the authorities of the Nationalist *Marina* (Navy) in the training tasks of their men at the *Escuela Naval* at San Fernando, Cadiz.

In any case, it was obviously Colonel Wilhelm *Ritter* von Thoma who was the most characterized chief of the German Army in Spain, both for the work carried out with the training of the Spaniards in the different areas of military science, and his later participation in the Second World War, which saw him in charges of major relevance until his premature capture by the British on African soil with Rommel's mythic *Afrika Korps*.

With this work, which digs deep into the particularities of the complex and little researched participation of the *Heer* in the Spanish Civil War, we want to pay a sincere tribute to all of those who certainly worked hard and relentlessly in the extremely difficult –and quite often thankless—task of training and consolidation of a real modern army, leaving aside ideologies and particular points of view, as their work was obviously superb.

And now, before we go into the substance of the work, we only have to thank heartily all of those who have actively contributed to this book, particularly Raúl Arias and José Manuel Campesino (for a large part of the accompanying pictures), Manolo Tamariz, Carlos Caballero, Carlos Díez, Juan Arráez, "Canario" Azaola, Carlos Murias, César O´Donnell, Eduardo Veguillas, and José Luis de Mesa.

To all of them, thanks.

The authors. Madrid, 27 August 2003

1

The *Heer* Goes to War

War in Spain

The failure of the mixed civil-cum-military coup in several of the *Divisiones Orgánicas* that the Spanish military territory was divided in on 18 July 1936 changed what should have been a rapid uprising into a cruel long civil war. The early moments were of obvious lack of coordination, both among the rebels and the republican authorities; sides began to mark out their boundaries, and commanders started to have real capacity to lead operations in each area, after the early days of the rebellion.

Precisely, as a side effect of this definition of sides, after those early days of incertitude, the only two units that had tanks (it would be an overstatement to call them "armored") in the Spanish Army those years were equally divided: one in Madrid, with the government forces, and the other one based at Saragossa, with the Nationalists. Both were equipped with the elderly worn-out Renault FT-17s armed with a 7-mm machine gun, from the acquisitions of the early twenties for the colonial war in Morocco. Five tanks for each side, that was all (apart from some Schneider CA-1s and Trubia A-4s). The figure was certainly negligible and obviously insufficient for modern warfare. It is logical that the Nationalists and Republicans tried to get some more of this combat equipment.

An event that took place in the first days of September 1936, in which there was no intervention by the rebel Army commanders, caused a substantial change in the military situation on the Nationalist side, in the conflict that had just started in Spain. This event has attracted little attention in the wide bibliography on the Spanish Civil War, but the point is, in our modest opinion, that it was decisive in the later developments, particularly the German help for the rebels on 18 July 1936.

Although it is true that German help—which materialized in the recent positive answer that the Reich leaders had given in the form of the support to the military uprising against the *Frente Popular*—had started to arrive in the Peninsula in the framework of Operation "Magic Fire," the arrival in Spain of *Oberstleutnant* Walter Warlimont, as chief of the German Military mission before Franco (main representative of the Reich until the official recognition by Germany) marked an inflexion, an important point of inflexion, in the material help for Nationalist Spain.

On 25 August, *General* Werner von Blomberg, head of the German Armed Forces (*Wehrmacht*) and Minister of War, summoned an unknown young Artillery officer called Warlimont to his office in Berlin.

The Brilliant Career of a Staff Officer

Walter Warlimont was born in Osnabrück, Germany, on 3 October 1894. Although his father was a publisher, he opted for a military career, entered the Artillery Academy, and started his service in the German Army in June 1914. During the First World War he fought on the Western front and commanded a battery, getting promoted several ranks.

Once the conflict was over, Warlimont took an active part in the *Freikorps* and remained in the new *Reichswehr*. In 1922 he was selected for a staff course and visited Britain (1926) and the USA (1929). As an *Oberstleutnant* of the *Heer*, he was sent to Spain in September 1936, and for a short time served as "representative of the *Wehrmacht* before Franco," i.e. a Military Attaché in Nationalist Spain. Besides his military education, Warlimont had a sound knowledge of Economy and Politics that allowed him to take up, in August 1936, the charge of director of the economic department of the *Heereswaffenamt* of the German Army (*Heer*). In addition to all these qualities, Warlimont was seen as a competent officer by his comrades, and of a solid and unshakeable character; it was precisely his career in that department that was one of the reasons why von Blomberg commended him for his mission in Spain, "the safeguard of German interests in the economic field"—in Abendroth's words.

Certainly, the man that was requested in that moment was an educated soldier who could act as a mediator between the rebel Spain and the powerful German Army, between Franco and the German General Staff, and with a peculiar characteristic, in that he should also have a good reputation in the social and political circles of the III Reich.

Oberstleutnant Walter Warlimont. He was the first German Military Attaché in Nationalist Spain. To a large extent, it is he who was responsible for the establishment of the *Panzer Gruppe Thoma* and the instructor teams created afterwards. His stay in Spain was very short, for he returned to Germany a few months later and left behind *Oberstleutnant* von Funk in the posting.

After a short stay in Spain, Warlimont returned to Germany in November 1936 because of some differences with Berlin. A month and a half later, he assumed command of the 26 Artillery Regiment, based in Düsseldorf.

In September 1938, Warlimont was posted to the *Oberkommando der Heer* (OKH), where he became *General* Alfred Jodl's right hand, atteding most of the conferences of the General Staff, and taking part in the drawing up of many operation plans and war directives. He was one of the officers who were seriously wounded in the attempt on Hitler's life in July 1944, and the sequels forced him to abandon active service in September that same year. In May 1945 he was arrested and judged in Nuremberg, where he was sentenced to 18-years in prison, but he only served eleven. When he was released in 1957, he wrote his memoirs, *Inside Hitler's Headquarters 1939/45*, where he made an exhaustive analysis of daily life in Hitler's headquarters during the convulsive years of the Second World War. Walter Warlimont died in Kreuth, Upper Bavaria, on 9 October 1976.

Walter Warlimont, the Chosen

Let's get back to 25 August 1936, when von Blomberg summoned Warlimont to his presence. Let's leave Warlimont himself to tell of his meeting with the German marshall:

"...By 25 August I was unexpectedly ordered to report to the top chief of the Armed Forces, Marshall von Blomberg, who, in a few words, told me more or less what follows: the conflict in Spain is assuming more complex forms, the Führer is willing to send, if necessary, more aid to General Franco... Italy will do the same. The volume of our support cannot be but limited, bearing in mind the state of our own rearmament. This help, in principle, should be in a way that General Franco was sent some war materiel, and should only include the presence of German personnel as far as they were needed to train the soldiers in the use of weapons.

The intervention of German troops in combat could only be considered in those cases where it was absolutely necessary and

General Alfred Jodl, head of the *Oberkommando der Heer*. He was convicted in Nuremberg and hanged in 1946. (via Raúl Arias)

Above left: *Admiral* Wilhelm Canaris, head of the German secret services (*Abwehr*). He had a deep knowledge of Spain and the idiosyncrasies of the Spanish people. (via Raúl Arias) Above right: *Generalfeldmarschall* Werner von Blomberg. He was the War Minister and commander in chief of the German Armed Forces in October 1936. He is wearing the *"Pour le Mérite,"* the top German decoration of the First World War. (J.M. Campesino via Raúl Arias)

after obtaining prior authorization. My mission was to act as representative of the German Armed Forces before General Franco, to watch over the interests of all those present in Spain and those that would come, to serve as adviser to General Franco as far as his likely wishes for more German help were concerned, based on my knowledge of the situation of our rearmament and on the circumstances that might prevail in Spain and, finally, taking into account that the military support for Spain should be repaid with the supply of Spanish raw materials." (Warlimont, W. *Die deutsche Beteiligung am spanischen Bürgerkrieg und einige spätere Folgerungen*, unpublished manuscript, reproduced in part in A. Viñas' work.)

The next day, 26 August, Warlimont met Admiral Canaris, chief of the *Abwher* and a deep connoisseur of Spain and the Spaniards, their idiosyncrasies and their customs. In his meeting with the latter, both prepared their imminent departure for Rome, where they should meet *generale* Mario Roatta to keep on working side by side with the Italians in the supply of military hardware to Spain. After that, Warlimont got back to Berlin and met *Generalleutnant* Helmuth Wilberg, chief of the recently established *Sonderstab* W, a Staff specially organized to coordinate German participation in the Spanish Civil War. Summing up, Warlimont's orders on 31 August were:

- Appointment by von Blomberg, Minister of War—in the *Führer's* name—as "representative before any command of the Armed Forces in Nationalist Spain."
- Assumption of these functions, "probably" on 3 September 1936.

These functions were specified in an annex to the document they were issued in before their departure for Spain and, basically, were as follows:

- To examine all the possibilities and proposals to support the Spanish Nationalists through the Spanish Armed Forces.
- To advise the Spanish Nationalist High Command.
- To safeguard German interests in areas such as political-military and economic affairs.
- To cooperate with the representatives of the Italian Forces in Spain.

(In Raymod Proctor's *Hitler's Luftwaffe in the Spanish Civil War*. 1983. Proctor interviewed Warlimont in 1976)

    One day after he got his instructions, Warlimont left again; now the destination was Rome to meet Roatta again, and afterwards both should go to the port of Gaeta and board a torpedo boat of the Italian *Marina* for Tangier. On the next day they left for Tétouan and thence, on a Junkers Ju 52, they flew to Seville, where they were welcomed by their first interlocutor in Nationalist Spain, General Queipo de Llano.

General de brigada Gonzalo Queipo de Llano, standing by *comandante* Castejón, haranguing the legionnaires in Seville in the early days of the uprising. Queipo was *Oberstleutnant* Warlimont's first interlocutor after the latter's arrival to Nationalist Spain.

On 6 September they were welcomed in Cáceres by General Franco, who had established his HQs in that town in Extremadura. Roatta introduced Warlimont to Franco, who handed him over the orders he had received from the latter's superior, von Blomberg.

Upon his arrival he relieved *Major* Alexander von Scheele at once, and established his HQs at the Hotel María Cristina, in Seville, making numerous trips in the territory in rebel hands, in order to analyze the operations and send reports to Berlin. As Germany had neither arms nor men officially involved in the Spanish conflict, *Oberstleutnant* Walter Warlimont used two pseudonyms during his stay in Spain: the best known was "Guido," although he also used "Woltersdorff" sporadically.

Reports to Berlin
The first report on the movements of the Nationalist forces during the early war months, as well as the Spaniards' use of the equipment so far delivered by Germany, was signed by Warlimont on 12 September. In the report, the *Oberstleutnant* clearly admitted Franco's leadership within the Military Junta in Burgos, an aspect on which Hitler had already got reliable information through a double channel, Canaris and Bernhardt. The former was the head of the *Abwher*, while the latter was one of the directors and co-founder of the HISMA Ltda. company.

As far as the evolution of the war was concerned, Warlimont recorded the good service rendered by the aircraft supplied by the *Luftwaffe* in the early stages of the combats, and in the passage of the Straits of Gibraltar by the rebel troops from Africa. However, the German lieutenant colonel was skeptical regarding the future of the military operations, as "reserves were running down." In his opinion, the conflict could only end quickly if Germany increased material help, mainly with armored vehicles or tanks and anti-aircraft and anti-tank guns—weapons that the Spaniards were in bad need of, as they had hardly any.

Warlimont asked Berlin to send an armored force, as well as anti-tank equipment, and was certainly surprised with the answer from Berlin, as the equipment eventually supplied was well beyond his hopes.

Johannes Bernhardt, founder of HISMA Ltda. and a key element for the German participation in the Spanish Civil War. (via Raúl Arias)

The German High Command approved the consignment of an armored force the size of a battalion, with a staff, two tank companies, a transport company, a workshop company, and an anti-tank and an armory training unit, whose command was entrusted to a pioneer of the German tank units, the then *Oberstleutnant* von Thoma.

On 23 September, the *Oberstleutnant* commanding the 2 Battalion of *Panzer Regiment* 4, based in Scheinfurt, i.e. Wilhelm Josef *Ritter* von Thoma, was sent to Spain. His mission, as defined by the *Heer* high command, was to take up command of the German armored group that was to embark a week later, destination: Spain.

In 1936, *Oberstleutnant* Wilhelm Josef *Ritter* von Thoma was the CO of the II *Battalion* of the 4.*Panzer-Regiment*, based in Scheinfurt as part of the 2.*Panzer-Division*. On 23 September 1936 he was posted as "Officer on special duties (Zbv)" and left for Spain to take over command of the land contingent of the *Legión Cóndor*.

He was the most characterized head of the *Heer* on Spanish soil during the Civil War, and his participation as head of the German instructors did not go unnoticed to the Spanish high command, which awarded him the *Medalla Militar Individual* at the end of the conflict.

He took part in the Second World War as commanding general of different armored units, although for him the war had an early end, for he was captured by the British on 4 November 1942 at Tel el Mampsra. (Bundesarchiv)

2

Panzergruppe Thoma

Introduction

Three days earlier, on 20 September 1936, all the officers, NCOs, and troops of the two battalions that made up *Panzer-Regiment* 6 were gathered at the Neuruppin base, and right there, the commanders asked for volunteers for a mission abroad of some relevance, but Spain was not mentioned. They warned their men that these were not just exercises or maneuvers; real fire was expected, and they could be made prisoners, wounded, or even get killed on the battlefield.

Almost every man stepped forward and volunteered for this secret mission outside their homeland; a romantic adventure for some, and a good chance to put into practice the tactics learned during long months for most of them. None of them knew of their end destination or the significance of the mission, but they knew for certain that it would not be an easy task.

With the personnel thus selected, the body of troops was organized and the standard type tanks in the unit at the time were prepared: forty-one *Panzerkampfwagen I Ausf. As*, apart from different types of vehicles, trucks, and motorcycles, as well as the armament that was necessary to fulfil the mission.

Note: the lowest rank allowed was that of *Gefreiter*, equivalent to a corporal in the Spanish Army; once in Spain, all of them were assimilated to sergeants.

The men of the second tank company of *Gruppe Thoma*, having a rest on the deck of the SS *Girgenti* on their way to Spain. (J.M. Campesino via Raúl Arias)

The SS *Girgenti*, one of the ships that took the German volunteers of the *Heer*, at sea. (J.M. Campesino via Raúl Arias)

The first volunteers (267 men) were taken to Döberitz, near Berlin, where they were given a bonus for urgent purchases and civil clothes. During the period of absence from Germany, they became temporarily excluded from the *Wehrmacht* so as not to jeopardize the presence of German soldiers supporting one of the contenders in the Spanish conflict.

The German tank crews, now wearing civil clothes and carrying false passports, made up a homogeneous group of German youth travelers waiting to board a ship to spend their summer holidays under the sun of a country they still knew nothing about. The group was driven to Stettin, a port town where they would board a ship, thinking their end destination was Danzig, a former German town that the *Reich* was claiming back from the Polish state.

On 28 September 1936, the members of the panzer unit boarded the SS *Pasajes* and the SS *Girgenti*, which were also carrying their impedimenta and all the necessary materiel for their task at destination.

The 267-man expedition was made up of the *Panzer Gruppe* Staff, two full tank companies, a transport company, a workshop company, and armory and anti-tank gun training units, with the following equipment: forty-one *Panzerkampfwagen I Ausf A* tanks, ten Büssing-NAG 80 trucks to tow tank carriers, six workshop trucks, eleven light cars, forty-five trucks (including fourteen Vomag tank carriers), nineteen low-axle *Sd. Ah. 115* tank carriers, and eighteen motorcycles, apart from twenty-four 37-mm *Pak 35/36* anti-tank guns and assorted accessories and spares.

The torpedo boat *Seeadler*, which escorted the steamers taking the two *Panzer Kompanien* to Spain. (J.M. Campesino via Raúl Arias)

On 7 October 1936 the ships reached Spanish waters, and from then on they were escorted by the battleships *Admiral Scheer* and *Deutschland* and the torpedo boat *Seeadler*. In the evening they moored in Seville, where the personnel and materiel were landed.

Although the *Panzer Gruppe* men were anxious to take the field, they were not sent to the front straightaway, as their main mission was to train Spanish soldiers in the handling of the tanks and their combat use and the tactical lessons learned in their country, of what modern armored war should be. Shortly after their arrival in Seville, they were sent to Cáceres by rail on several trips, between 8 and 10 October. A week later, on the 18th, Franco reviewed the troops at their base, at Las Herguijuelas castle.

By then, *Oberstleutnant* von Thoma had already assumed command of the unit, with *Maj* Eberhardt von Ostman as Chief-of-Staff.

During November, a further thirty-seven men joined them and, along with some of their comrades already in Spain and a further twenty-one tanks—in this case *Panzerkampfwagen I Ausf Bs* that arrived in Seville on the 25th on the SS *Urania*, from *Panzer Regiment 4*—made up the 3rd Tank Company of the *Panzer Gruppe*, commanded by *Hauptm* Karl Ernst Bothe. Also, the *Panzer Gruppe* command post moved to Cubas de la Sagra, Madrid, where the Training School and workshops were also established.

One of the large Vomag trucks —with a *Panzerkampfwagen I Ausf. A* on it— towing an Sd.Ah. 115 tank transport platform with another of the same type. (J.M. Campesino via Raúl Arias)

The second tank company of *Gruppe Thoma* at full strength. In the middle is its CO, *Hauptmann* Wolf, and the deputy CO, *Oberleutnant* Willing. Notice the first type of uniform used by the German tank crews in Spain. (J.M. Campesino via Raúl Arias)

On 31 December 1936 *Gruppe Thoma* was thus organized:

Group CO   Col Wilhelm von Thoma (23/09/36-31/05/39)
Staff 35 members
    Unit CO: Lt Col Eberhard von Ostman (08/10/36-29/08/37)
    Doctor: Maj Johannes Engelhardt (08/10/36-01/08/37)
    Quartermaster: Maj Fritz Muehlenkamp (08/10/36-15/05/37)
    Members: 4 2/Lts, 18 W/Os, 9 Sgts and 1 interpreter
1 Tank Company   65 members
    Company CO: Maj Joachim Ziegler (08/10/36-18/03/38)
    Deputy Coy CO: Capt Ferdinand von Planitz (08/10/36-28/09/37)
    Section CO: Lt Erwin Strauchmann (08/10/36-20/07/37)
    Members: 7 2/Lts, 43 W/Os, 9 Sgts, 1 medical attendant and 2 interpreters
2 Tank Company   66 members
    Company CO: Maj Heinz Wolf (08/10/36-25/07/37)
    Deputy Coy CO: Capt Gerhard Willing (08/10/36-14/09/37)
    Section CO: Lt Hannibal von Moerner (08/10/36-24/07/37) KIA
    Members: 7 2/Lts, 44 W/Os, 9 Sgts, 1 medical attendant and 2 interpreters
3 Tank Company   64 members (Established 06-12-1936)
    Company CO: Maj Karl-Ernst Bothe (01/11/36-16/12/37)
    Deputy Coy CO: Lt Karl Pfannkuche (01/11/36-06/12/37)
    Section CO: Lt Ottfried Sanfft von Pilsa (01/10/36-15/10/37)
    Members: 6 2/Lts, 43 W/Os, 9 Sgts, 1 medical attendant and 2 interpreters
Transport Company   36 members
    Company CO: Capt Hans Schruefer (08/10/36-31/05/39)
    Members: 6 2/Lts, 18 W/Os, 9 Sgts, 2 mechanics
Workshop Company   23 members
    Company CO: Capt Albert Schneider (01/11/36-31/05/39)
    Workshop CO: Lt Paul Jaskula (08/10/36-30/04/37) Killed in air crash
    Members: 1 2/Lt, 8 W/Os, 10 mechanics and 2 interpreters
Anti-tank Training Unit 9 members
    Unit CO: Maj Peter Jansa(01/11/36-18/03/38)
    Members: 3 2/Lts, 4 W/Os and 1 interpreter
Armoury   6 members
    Members: 2 2/Lts, 3 W/Os and 1 armourer
Interpreters   2 Group interpreters, subordinated to the *Legión Cóndor*

Total: 307 members arrived September to December 1936

Note: the ranks in the table were those the Germans had in Spain, which, as we have seen, were one immediately above their rank in Germany. Beside the names of the COs cited, arrival dates in Spain and departure or death are noted where applicable.

Excellent view of Las Herguijuelas Castle, Cáceres, first location of the tank unit established by Wilhelm *Ritter* von Thoma and his instructors of the *Gruppe Thoma*. (J.M. Campesino via Raúl Arias)

The *Gruppe Thoma* tank instructors trained their Spanish pupils, among other disciplines, in the use, assembly, and cleaning of armament. In the picture, a practice class on the Dreyse MG-13 machine gun, fitted to the German *Panzerkampfwagen I* tanks. (J.M. Campesino via Raúl Arias)

Several members of the *Drohne* at work with the armament and ammunition of a panzer. (J.M. Campesino via Raúl Arias)

Top: *Oberleutnant* Willing, 2.*Kompanie*, standing by a group of Spanish tank crewmen. In the early days, the German instructors' uniforms lacked homogeneity, in this case a civilian's cap. In the background, one of the first *Panzer I* tanks that arrived in Cáceres. (J.M. Campesino via Raúl Arias) Bottom: the Dreyse MG-13 machine gun was a 7.92-mm automatic weapon, made by Rheinische Metallwaren und Machinenfabrik. (J.M. Campesino via Raúl Arias)

Between October and December 1936, eight casualties were recorded in *Grupppe Thoma*: seven tank instructors and a staff member. Of them, two instructors were killed/died in accidents on the front, and the rest returned to Germany on different grounds. For that reason, by late 1936 there were only two hundred and ninety-nine tank crewmen of the *Heer* left in Spain.

Out of these two hundred and ninety-nine tank crewmen of *Gruppe Thoma* that remained in Spain on 31 December 1936, 270 left for Germany or were killed/died during 1937, and ninety-five new members arrived from Germany as replacements for the group. Besides, there were forty-five posting changes among the different units of the *Panzergruppe*. Thus, on 31 December 1937 there were only one hundred and twenty-four German tank crewmen left in Spain. Let's see its composition on that date:

	01/01/37	Joined	Left	31/12/37
Drohne CO	1	-	1	
Staff[7]	34	29 (+2) (+1)	33	33
Tank Companies[1, 3, 5, 8]	188	35	169 (+18) (+1)	35
Transport Company[4, 9]	36	13	37 (+2)	10
Workshop Company[2, 6]	23	4	19 (+1)	7
Anti-tank Training Unit	9	5	6	8
Armoury	6	6	6	6
Interpreters	2	1	-	3
Infantry Academies	-	2 (+41) (+1)	23	21
TOTAL	299	95 (+45)	270 (+45)	124

Oberst Eberhardt von Ostman during the Second World War. He is wearing several decorations gained in the 1936/39 war on his German uniform. (Bundesarchiv)

(1) In June 1937, a tank instructor 2/Lt joined the Workshop, although he left for Germany four months later. Thus, it is considered here as struck off charge as a tank instructor.

(2) In July 1937, a Workshop W/O joined the Staff and left for Germany four months later. It is considered here as struck off charge from the Workshop.

(3) In June 1937, a tank instructor 2/Lt joined the Staff, and remained in Spain until May 1939. It is considered here as struck off charge from a tank company and as a Staff enrolment.

(4) Two W/Os that arrived in the Transport Company during 1937 joined the Staff before year's end. Thus, they are considered here as struck off charge from the Transport Company and as Staff enrolments.

(5) Forty-one tank company members that arrived 1936 to 1937 became instructors in the Infantry Academies April to July 1937 (two of them were Co COs), so they are considered here as struck off charge as tank instructors that year and Infantry Academies enrolments. Of them, twenty-three left for Germany that same year. Thus, only eighteen remained in Spain after 12-31-37. These eighteen are considered here as struck off charge from tank companies that year.

(6) In May 1937, a Workshop W/O became an instructor in the Infantry Academies, and remained in Spain until 1939. It is considered here as struck off charge from the Workshop and as an Infantry Instructor enrolment.

(7) In May 1937, three Staff members became instructors in the Infantry Academies but left for Germany that same year. They are thus considered here as struck off charge from the Staff.

(8) In June 1937 a tank instructor W/O became an anti-tank Instructor, although shortly afterwards, in October, he left Spain. It is considered here as struck off charge as a tank instructor.

(9) A Transport Company Sgt joined the Staff on 12-01-37 and left for Germany a fortnight later. It is considered here as struck off charge from the Transport Company.

Four of "von Thoma's men" at Cubas, 1937. (J.M. Campesino via Raúl Arias)

Sgt Otto Maurer, of the *Drohne* Staff, playing the accordion on a "stylish steed." (J.M. Campesino via Raúl Arias)

The two crewmen of a *Panzer I*, in their brand new uniforms and the tank crews' black beret, posing in front of their vehicle, camouflaged with assorted vegetation. (J.M. Campesino via Raúl Arias)

The members of *Panzer Gruppe Thoma* were unmistakable for the use of the black beret in conjunction with elegant beige uniform and leather straps. (J.M. Campesino via Raúl Arias)

Left to right, *Leutnant* Hannibal von Moerner, *Oberleutnant* Gerhard Willing, and *Unteroffizier* Hans Joachim Freitag. (J.M. Campesino via Raúl Arias)

Through the stone gate, and next to the Germans' tents, a *Panzerkampfwagen I Ausf A* is driving away. (J.M. Campesino via Raúl Arias)

One of the conical tents where the members of *Gruppe Thoma* stayed in the area surrounding Las Herguijuelas Castle, Cáceres. (J.M. Campesino via Raúl Arias)

The castle gate. (J.M. Campesino via Raúl Arias)

Germans and Spaniards sharing outer guard missions at the Nationalist tank base, Las Herguijuelas Castle. (J.M. Campesino via Raúl Arias)

Several members of the *Drohne* sitting in front of their tent. Left, standing, the sentry with his Mauser. (J.M. Campesino via Raúl Arias)

Sgt Horst Muchow on guard duties at Cubas, taking protection from the cold Spanish winter with a great coat, and the tireless 7.92-mm Mauser across his shoulders. (J.M. Campesino via Raúl Arias)

Hauptmann Heinz Wolf, CO of the *2ª Compañía de Carros* of *Gruppe Thoma*. He stayed in Spain until 25 July 1937. (J.M. Campesino via Raúl Arias)

18 October 1936: Franco, just appointed Generalissimo of the Nationalist Armies, paying a visit to the volunteers of *Gruppe Thoma* in their provisional quartering at Las Herguijuelas Castle, Cáceres. In the picture are Franco and *Oberstleutnant* Wilhelm von Thoma. The latter is wearing rather Spartan overalls that he often used to wear during the first part of his stay in Spain. No badge is visible on the black beret yet. (J.M. Campesino via Raúl Arias)

Franco, von Thoma, Barroso, and some other Germans and Spaniards during the visit of the former to the German tank contingent. (J.M. Campesino via Raúl Arias)

Two views showing the loading of a *Panzer I Ausf A* on a Vomag special truck. Fourteen of these trucks were supplied, along with another ten Büssing-NAGs and eighteen Sd.Ah.15 tank transport trailers. (J.M. Campesino via Raúl Arias)

Top: shelter at Asua (Bilbao front). Left, Spanish *alférez médico* Manuel de Cuadros. Right, *Stabsarzt* (medical captain) Dr. Johannes Engelhardt. This was the chief medical officer of *Gruppe Thoma*. He was in Spain from October 1936 to 1 August 1937, when he was replaced by *Stabsarzt* Dr. Hans Rossner. Bottom: the last positions of the *cinturón de hierro* defense line around Bilbao, after their capture by the Nationalist infantry on 18 June 1937. (J.M. Campesino via Raúl Arias)

Top: members of *Panzer Gruppe Drohne* inspecting anti-tank trenches at Gózquez (Jarama front). The *Panzer Is* of the Nationalist *Batallón de Carros* were intensively used on all the operations around the river Jarama, sustaining the total loss of two tanks (captured by the enemy) and another nine knocked out. Bottom: two *Panzer I Bs* at Alar de Rey, Palencia, August 1937. (J.M. Campesino via Raúl Arias)

Top: a *Panzer I Ausf A* of the *2ª Compañía*, with a sucking pig for dinner and a bicycle on the rear. Bottom: W/O Knobloch refuelling a *Panzerkampfwagen I Ausf A*. (J.M. Campesino via Raúl Arias)

The Spanish units

The purpose of the presence of *Panzer-Gruppe Thoma* in Spain was none other than the training of the Nationalist troops in the battlefield use of the *Panzerkampfwagen I* and the special vehicles of the transport unit and the workshops, as well as assorted materiel supplied by the "*negrillos*,"[2] such as anti-tank guns, flame-throwers, etc.

A Spanish tank battalion had been established with personnel from the *Regimiento de Infantería "Argel" nº 37* in Cáceres on 1 October. A week later, the unit was organized under the command of retired Infantry *comandante*[3] José Pujales, who had once served in the Renault FT-17-equipped *Compañía de Carros Ligeros de Asalto* (Light Tank Company), and was thus highly experienced in the training and use of armored equipment.

The Spaniards organized their unit using the German one that had just arrived in Cáceres as a model: a Staff, two tank companies, a transport unit, a workshop company,, and an anti-tank company. *Capitán* José García García, from the Spanish Foreign Legion, was appointed commander of the *1ª Compañía de Carros*, and *capitán* Juan García García was given the command of the *2ª Compañía*.

Comandante José Pujales Carrasco, head of the Nationalist *Batallón de Carros*, interpreter (*Dolmetscher*) Heinrich Winkler, and *Hauptmann* Heinz Wolf, head of the German training *2ª Compañía*. The permanent living together of the Germans with the Spanish created intense bonds. (J.M. Campesino via Raúl Arias)

On 1 December, when a new company of German tanks joined in, the Spanish *3ª Compañía* was also established at Cubas, commanded by Infantry *capitán* Gonzalo Díez de la Lastra Peralta.

On 1 October 1937, another *Panzer I* company was established at Casarrubuelos (number 5, and belonging to the so-called *2º Grupo*), commanded by Infantry *capitán* Pedro Jiménez, and equipped with sixteen new tanks out of the thirty that had arrived from Germany by early September. In the composition of the *Primer Batallón de Carros de Combate* (1st Tank Battalion), this company was called the *5ª Compañía de Negrillos*, probably to distinguish it from those equipped with T-26 B tanks, which were called "*rusas.*"[4]

On 14 October 1937, in order to establish two new companies equipped with gun-armed tanks, the Generalissimo's HQs ordered *general* Orgaz to send, once repaired, all the Renault and Trubia tanks captured in the North. Indeed, during the Santander campaign a total of thirteen Renault tanks and three Trubia tanks (these were certainly the Trubia-Naval tanks, called "*carro Euzkadi*"[5] in numerous books) and two Trubia-Landesa tanks (these might have been two Landesa armored tractors) had been captured, as shown in the table below. All of them were sent by the *Servicio de Recuperación* to the *Fábrica de Artillería* in Seville for rebuilding, and at least ten of them were repaired and sent to Saragossa, to *Regimiento de Carros nº 2.*

Tanks recovered on the Santander front

Date	Type or class	Recovered at	Sent to	Condition
24-08-37	3 Renault	Matabecausera	Seville	1 armed
25-08-37	2 " "	Reinosa road	Armed	
26-08-37	3 " "	Montes Claros		Good, 1 armed
26-08-37	1 " "	Santueno		Scrapped
26-08-37	1 " "	Torrelavega-Oviedo crossroad		Unarmed
01-09-37	2 Trubia-Landesa	Guarnizo		Good, unarmed
07-09-37	3 Renault	Salaya (Puerto)		2 armed, 1 unarmed
12-09-37	2 Trubia	Muriedas		Armed
16-09-37	1 Trubia	Santander Depot		Good, unarmed

A.G.M. (Ávila) C.G.G. 12/593/22/19

All of them, along with those recovered in Asturias that joined another ten Renaults, were used to reinforce the *Carros Renault* section, which had been operating on the Aragón front commanded by Infantry *alférez*[6] Alejandro Arruga.

So as to avoid confusion with the different fusilier battalions that the *Regimiento de Carros de Combate nº 2* organized during the campaign, on 1 October 1937 the "*negrillo*" tank battalion became the *Primer Batallón de Carros de Combate*, which saw a modification of its composition on that date, now with two tank *Grupos* with three companies each: two made up of German *Panzer Is*, and one with Russian T-26 tanks, apart from other independent units with the following composition:

- Battalion Command and Staff: *Teniente Coronel* José Pujales Carrasco
- First Group: Command and Staff: *Capitán* Gonzalo Díez de la Lastra.
  1ª and 2ª *Cías. de Carros Negrillos.* 3ª *Cía.[7] de Carros Rusos.*
- Second Group: Command and Staff: *Comandante* Modesto Sáez de Cabezón.
  4ª and 5ª *Cías. de Carros Negrillos.* 6ª *Cía. de Carros Renault* (in the process of being replaced with Russian T-26s)
  Starting from the 18 November on, it came under the control of the Spaniards, a measure that was taken because of the hardening of the war, which made the Germans see the dangers of getting too involved in operations. Then they handed the unit over.
- Anti-tank Gun Company
- Transport Company: *Capitán* José Alfaro Páramo.
- Workshop Company: *Capitán* Félix Verdeja Bardales.
  For the same reason, starting from 1 November on it was handed over to Spanish personnel.

A member of the *Legión Cóndor* closely watching some Renault FT-17 tanks captured in Santander in August 1937. In this campaign, the Nationalists managed to recover thirteen tanks of this type, in better or worse condition. They were obsolete and, although they were sent to Seville for repairs, they were not used much by the *Batallón de Carros*, which grouped them in a rearguard company for training. (J.M. Campesino via Raúl Arias)

Capitán José Losada Vera, CO of the Spanish *2ª Compañía* of *"negrillo"* tanks with *Oberleutnant* Willing, deputy CO of the *2.Panzer-Kompanie* of *Gruppe Thoma*. (J.M. Campesino via Raúl Arias)

Left to right: *Obltn.* Willing, *Cmte.* Pujales, *Oberstltn.* von Thoma, *Gen. der Fl.* Sperrle, and *Obltn.* Aldinger (Flak 88/56) at Derio. (J.M. Campesino via Raúl Arias)

A BT-5 tank of Soviet origin captured by the Nationalists. The armored forces of the Republic had a battalion armed with these tanks, which did not meet expectations. (Avila General Military Archives)

(via Juan Arráez Cerdá)

Panzer Drohne in 1938

Once the year 1937 was over, and after the changes, arrivals, and departures of German personnel, *Panzer Gruppe Thoma* was organized as follows and with this strength:

Group CO	Col Wilhelm von Thoma (23/09/36-31/05/39)
Staff	33 members
Doctor:	Capt Hans Roessner (01/07/37-09/04/38)
Quartermaster:	Capt Max Franzbach (01/05/37-31/05/39)
Members:	2 2/Lts, 23 W/Os, 5 Sgts and 1 interpreter
Tank Company	35 members
Company CO:	Maj Herbert Crohn (01/11/37-31/05/39)
Section COs:	Lt H. Joachim Falkenberg von H. (01/11/37-02/05/38)
	Lt Axel von Levetzow (01/11/37-31/05/039)
	Lt Ernst Fremm (01/11/37-31/05/39)
Members:	2 2/Lts, 21 W/Os, 2 Sgts, 3 medical attendants and 3 interpreters
Transport Company	10 members
Company CO:	Capt Hans Schruefer (08/10/36-31/05/39)
Members:	1 2/Lt, 5 W/Os, 1 Sgt and 2 mechanics
Workshop Company	7 members
Company CO:	Capt Albert Schneider (01/11/36-31/05/39)
Members:	5 W/Os and 1 interpreter
Anti-tank Training Unit	8 members
Unit CO:	Maj Peter Jansa(01/11/36-18/03/38)
Members:	2 2/Lts, 3 W/Os, 1 Sgt and 1 interpreter
Armory	6 members
Members:	3 2/Lts, 2 W/Os and 1 armorer
Interpreters	3 Group interpreters, subordinated to the *Legión Cóndor*

Top: The vehicles of the *Panzer Gruppe Drohne* had registration plates with the group emblem, a skull and two tibias crossed. Bottom: a *"negrillo" Panzerkampfwagen I Ausf A* tank at the square of a village that has just been captured. The sequels of the combats are pretty visible in the picture. (both J.M. Campesino via Raúl Arias)

Top: the captain in command of the workshop company, Albert Schneider (right), standing by the workshop CO, 1/Lt Paul Jaskula (left). By his side, one of the *Panzer I Ausf As* destroyed on the Madrid front by early 1937. Bottom: close-up of the condition of the tank in the upper picture. The German workshop at Cubas was a most important element in the composition of *Gruppe Thoma*. Its men were the real force behind the operational readiness of the German armored equipment. (both J.M. Campesino via Raúl Arias)

The *Panzer Drohne* as such thus totalled just one hundred and twenty-four members on 1 January 1938, of which only one hundred and three served in the tank unit, as twenty-one of them were assigned to the different Infantry academies as instructors.

Obviously, once the year 1937 was over, and once the four "*negrillo*" tank companies in the Nationalist Army had been established, the contingent that made up the tank instructors' composition the year before (one hundred and ninety-five men) was reduced to just thirty-five, and their only task was to maintain and support the whole of the Spanish units on the front. Besides, the transport and workshop companies were handed over to the Spaniards in November 1937, for which reason their composition, just as it had happened with the instructors, was substantially reduced: the Transport Company was left with ten, and the Workshop Company with seven. The Staff, the Anti-tank Training Unit, and the Armory remained more or less with the same strength as the year before.

The year 1938 was calmer as regards the *Drohne* personnel changes. The following table shows the arrivals, departures, and posting changes of the one hundred and twenty-four members that were left on 1 January 1938:

	1-1-38	Joined	Left	31-12-38
Drohne CO	1	-	-	1
Staff	33	19(+1)	14	39
Tank Companies (4)	35	3	17	21
Transport Company (1)	10	-	1(+1)	8
Workshop Company	7	1	1	7
Anti-tank Training Unit	8	-	1	7
Armory	6	1	1	6
Interpreters (2)	3	-	3	0
Infantry academies (3)	21	-	2	19
TOTAL	124	24(+1)	40(+1)	108

Panzer Gruppe Drohne had a total of 71 light, medium, and heavy cars, including Wanderer W-11s, like this one. (J.M. Campesino via Raúl Arias)

(1)   In January 1938, a Transport Company 2/Lt and a W/O joined the Staff; the former left for Germany four months later, and the latter stayed in Spain until May 1939. Both are considered here as struck off charge from the Transport Company in 1938, although the latter is considered as a Staff enrolment.

(2)   In January 1938, the three *Legión Cóndor* interpreters attached to the Panzer Group became Artillery Instructors. They are considered here as struck off charge as interpreters and as Artillery instructor enrolments.

(3)   Two Infantry Instructors from the tank companies left for Germany during 1938.

(4)   *Oberleutnant* Gustav Trippe joined the tank company on 1 March 1938. Unfortunately, he was KIA on 14 November that same year, during the Ebro battle, at the Fatarella Sierra.

A member of the *Drohne* standing by an Auto-Union vehicle of the contingent. The skull in the middle of the registration plates allotted it to the *Gruppe*, and the L C letters denoted the *Legión Cóndor*. (J.M. Campesino via Raúl Arias)

Wilhelm *Ritter* von Toma, wearing the colonel's uniform of *Gruppe Drohne*, standing with his second-in-command and head of the *Gruppe* staff, *Oberstleutnant* Eberhardt von Ostman. The former remained in Spain continuously for almost the three years of conflict; the latter, after serving in the staff until 30 April 1937, became head instructor at the Infantry academies and returned to Germany on 30 August that same year. (J.M. Campesino via Raúl Arias)

One of the rare pictures depicting a *Panzerbefehlswagen I Ausf.B* command tank of the *Agrupación de Carros de La Legión*. Notice the most interesting camouflage scheme in ochre and green. (Raúl Arias Collection)

Top: a *Panzerkampfwagen I Ausf. A* towing a Soviet T-26 B tank, called "Vickers" in Spain. The huge numbers of this tank type captured by the Nationalists allowed *Gruppe Thoma* instructors to have two of them at the school at Cubas de la Sagra to train the Spanish troops. (J.M. Campesino via Raúl Arias) Bottom: a *Drohne* instructor shows a Spanish soldier how to homogenize the machine guns of a *Panzer I Ausf A* in the workshop at Cubas. (Authors)

UNL-35 light armored car, also known as "Unión Naval de Levante" or LAV. This is a vehicle of the seventh series built in which the front mudguards were sloped outwards and the front machine gun gunner had an aiming orifice. The armored forces of the Republic numbered over 150 units, many of which were captured—like the one in the picture—by the Nationalists. (J.M. Campesino via Raúl Arias)

A member of *Gruppe Thoma* poses in front of a "Bilbao" Modelo 1932 armored car captured from the Republicans on the Madrid front. These Spanish made vehicles were standard for the *Guardia de Asalto* and the *Grupo de Autoametralladoras de Caballería* before the war. Most of them stayed in the area controlled by the Popular Front. (J.M. Campesino via Raúl Arias)

BA-6 heavy armored car. These were modern Soviet armored cars—the first ones rolled out of the factory in 1935—supplied to the Republicans. They were fitted with the same turret as the T-26 B tank, with a powerful 45-mm M-1932 gun and two Degtyarev DT-1932 machine guns. The Nationalists captured several of these vehicles, and enlisted them into the tank units. (J.M. Campesino via Raúl Arias)

(Authors)

The Spanish tank units during 1938
The tank unit kept on operating as the *Primer Batallón de Carros de Combate* until February 1938, but in order to avoid the administrative problems caused by the diverse origins of the personnel, and in order to give an economic and prestige incentive by qualifying them as "storm troops" since 12 February 1938, the Generalissimo's HQs decreed the administrative transfer, on official letter no 4,745, of all the personnel of the *Primer Batallón de Carros de Combate* to the Spanish *Legión*. Two weeks later, it was entirely under the command of the *2° Tercio de la Legión*,[8] designated as the *Bandera de Carros de Combate de la Legión*,[9] with the following composition:

- *Bandera* Command and Staff: *Teniente coronel* Pujales
- *Primer Grupo* Command and Staff: *Comandante* Díaz de la Lastra.
     1ª and 2ª *Cías. de Carros Negrillos*. 3ª *Cía. de Carros Rusos*
- *Segundo Grupo*: Command and Staff: *Comandante* José García García
     4ª and 5ª *Cías. de Carros Negrillos*. 6ª *Cía. de Carros Rusos* (former *Cía. de Carros Renault*)
- Anti-tank Gun Company: *Capitán* Martín Ercilla García
- Transport Company: *Capitán* José Alfaro Páramo
- Workshop Company: *Capitán* Félix Verdeja Bardales
- Tank School (Casarrubuelos, Madrid): *Capitán* La Cruz Lacacci
- *Cía. de Carros Renault* (obsolete equipment and in very bad need of spares)
- Depot Unit

On 1 October, because of the ever-growing dimensions of the operations theatre, the *grupos* (groups) making up the *Bandera de Carros de Combate* scaled up their size, and so they were supplied with rearguard repair echelons and saw their personnel figures strengthened. These *grupos* became *batallones* (battalions), and the units of the *Bandera de Carros de Combate* not included in the *grupos* remained with the same designation and composition, except for the Workshop Company, which was considerably reinforced and often supported by the Vickers mobile workshops. As a result of these changes, the *Bandera de Carros de Combate de la Legión* became the *Agrupación de Carros de Combate de la Legión*, a designation that was kept to the end of the conflict. Its organization was as follows:

Top: "Russian" tank section, assigned to a tank company of the Nationalist Army. (Authors)
Next page, top: a T-26 B captured by the Nationalists and enlisted into their tank units. The front of the turret was painted in the colors of the national (monarchist) flag. (via Juan Arráez Cerdá)
Next page, bottom: a mobile tank repair workshop. (Avila General Military Archives)

- *Agrupación*[10] Command and Staff: *Teniente coronel habilitado*[11] Díez de la Lastra
- *Primer Batallón* Command and Staff: *Capitán* Maximiliano Galiana Castilla
    1ª and 2ª *Cías. de Carros Negrillos*. 3ª *Cía. de Carros Rusos*
    Workshops
- *Segundo Batallón* Command and Staff: *Comandante* José García García.
    4ª and 5ª *Cías. de Carros Negrillos*. 6ª *Cía. de Carros Rusos*
    Workshops
- Anti-tank Company (37-mm guns): *Capitán* Martín Ercilla García
- Transport Company: *Capitán* José Alfaro Páramo
- Workshop Company: *Capitán* Félix Verdeja Bardales
- *Cía. de Carros Renault* (obsolete equipment and in very bad need of spares)
- Depot Unit

Top: officers of a Nationalist tank company in late 1938. The black beret, as it happened with their German mates, identified them as members of the tank units of the Army, a tradition that has remained to this day. (Authors)

Bottom: T-26 B n° 638, of the *6ª Compañía* of the *II Batallón* of the *Agrupación de Carros de Combate de La Legión*. On the mudguard, the yoke and arrows, the emblem of the *Falange Española*; on the front, the tank number (638) and on the vertical part of the glacis, the emblem of *La Legión* and a white circle (*6ª Cía*). (via Juan Arráez Cerdá)

(J.M. Campesino via Raúl Arias)

The Last Months of *Panzer Gruppe Thoma*
By early 1939, the composition of von Thoma's German tank group had been slimmed down even further to one hundred and eight members in the following manner:

Group CO   Col Wilhelm von Thoma (23/09/36-31/05/39)
Staff   39 members
             Doctor: Maj Hermann Essebruegge (01/03/38-31/05/39)
             Quartermaster: Capt Max Franzbach (01/05/37-31/05/39)
             Members: 3 2/Lts, 21 W/Os, 12 Sgts and 1 interpreter
Tank Company   21 members
             Company CO: Maj Herbert Crohn (01/11/37-31/05/39)
             Section COs: Lt Axel von Levetzow (01/11/37-31/05/39)
             Lt Ernst Fremm (01/11/37-31/05/39)
             Members: 2 2/Lts, 11 W/Os, 2 medical attendants and 3 interpreters
Transport Company   8 members
             Company CO: Capt Hans Schruefer (08/10/36-31/05/39)
             Members: 4 W/Os, 1 Sgt and 2 mechanics
Workshop Company   7 members
             Company CO: Capt Albert Schneider (01/11/36-31/05/39)
             Members: 4 W/Os, 1 Sgt and 1 interpreter
Anti-tank Training Unit 7 members
             Members: 2 2/Lts, 3 W/Os, 1 Sgt and 1 interpreter
Armory 6 members
             Members: 3 2/Lts, 2 W/Os and 1 armorer
Infantry Instructors   19 members

The capture of Soviet T-26 B tanks by the Nationalist troops and their rapid overhaul by the *Maestranza de Artillería* in Seville were extremely important to increase the power of the tank units. In the picture, two members of the *Legión Cóndor* are watching a T-26 B of the *Bandera de Carros de La Legión*. (Juan Arráez Cerdá)

In total, the *Panzer Drohne* was reduced to one hundred and eight members, who remained in Spain until the end of the conflict.

From their arrival in Spain in October 1936 until their departure in May 1939, von Thoma's men instructed Spanish personnel on matters that as diverse as tanks, anti-tank guns, flame throwers, mine throwers, gas protection, and workshop or armory masters. With Telegram no 1414 from the Generalissimo's HQs, dated in Burgos on 20 April 1938 and sent to the general director of *Movilización, Instrucción y Recuperación*,[12] Franco sent Orgaz a résumé copy of the training task carried out by von Thoma's group from 1 October 1936 until late March 1938. This document, so far unpublished and of enormous importance both in details and quantities, remarkably increases the figures of "Spaniards trained," which so far only included those who were trained at some of the officer or temporary warrant officer academies, but never those we are showing below.

Picking up the information from the abovementioned document, this is the table that can be drawn up:

Spanish Personnel trained by *Gruppe Thoma* until March 1938

Category	Officers	Sergeants	Soldiers
German tanks	33	434 (both categories)	
Russian tanks	4	141 (both categories)	
Spanish anti-tank guns	89	211	1,549
Vehicle 69 (Krupp Protze)	30 drivers		
Italian anti-tank guns	10	32	79
Flame throwers	7	239 (both categories)	
Tank transport on heavy trucks	1	75 diesel drivers	
7.7 cm mine throwers	177	220	2,000
7.7 cm field guns	30	80	500
Gas protection	180 officers, Sgts and soldiers*		
Workshop	1 master and 20 mechanics		
Tank & anti-tank armourer masters	2 masters, 56 master aides		
Total personnel trained	6,200 men		

* Besides, they trained the *8ª Bandera de La Legión* and the Chemical Warfare Section of the *Fábrica de Armas de Toledo*—Toledo Arms Factory.

Panzer Gruppe Thoma, with its officers, warrant officers, and technicians' team, also cared for the following units on the different battlefronts where they operated:

-4 German tank companies, 16 tanks each
-2 Russian tank companies, 22 tanks (March 1938)
-20 anti-tank gun companies, 10 guns each.

The CO of the workshop, 1/Lt Paul Jaskula, with his team inside the hangar in front of a *Panzer I B*. In the background, notice the *Panzerbefehlswagen I B* fitted with a curious element used at the tank workshop, a U-shaped brace fitted in the rear of the tank itself, used to remove the engine of a *Panzer I* by means of a system of pulleys and riggings. (J.M. Campesino via Raúl Arias)

Top: left, two members of the *Drohne* Workshop at work. Right: several members of the *Drohne* with a *Regulares* soldier looking through binoculars. (J.M. Campesino via Raúl Arias)
Bottom: a Moorish soldier handing out a light to the CO of the *2ª Compañía* of *Panzer Gruppe Drohne*. (J.M. Campesino via Raúl Arias)

3

German Tanks and Anti-Tank Guns in Spain

Much has been written on the tanks supplied by Germany to the Nationalist side during the Spanish conflict, from well-researched works, backed up by the accuracy and prestige of the authors, to real nonsense that would make any serious researcher ashamed. Maybe too many works have been published, but certainly few have managed to determine the real amount of German armored contribution to the Spanish Civil War.

In a previous work ("*Legión Cóndor. La historia olvidada*"), the authors unveiled the total figures of tanks supplied to the *Gruppe Thoma* through the *Legión Cóndor*, i.e. the tanks supplied by Germany to the land contingent for organization and operations at the beginning of the conflict during 1936: they numbered seventy-two, which arrived in Spain in three separate shipments of forty-one, twenty-one, and ten tanks respectively.

The first shipment of forty tanks of the *Panzerkampfwagen I* type arrived on the SS *Pasajes* and SS *Girgenti* in October 1936, along with the personnel and the rest of the materiel, and all of them were used to establish the first units of the Nationalist *Batallón de Carros de Combate*. Although the documents do not record any specific mention regarding these tanks, it is logical to think that they included at least three command tanks: one for the battalion, and another two (one each) for each of the companies established.

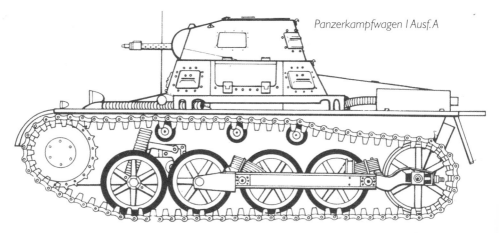

Panzerkampfwagen I Ausf. A

After their arrival in Seville on the SS *Girgenti* and *Pasajes*, the *Panzerkampfwagen I Ausf. As* were sent to Cáceres by rail.

The German tanks, contrary to what has been sustained so far, arrived in a three-color camouflage that was typical in Germany during those years, as shown in this photograph. (J.M. Campesino via Raúl Arias)

These tanks were used to equip two full companies, of three sections with five tanks each, and one for the company CO, which made a total of thirty-three tanks, i.e. thirty combat and three command tanks. As regards the eight remaining, one was for driver training, of the type called "*ohne Aufbau*" in Germany, i.e. without upper structure or turret, used on driving courses. The other seven were kept as reserves to make up the expected combat losses of the unit, later to be assigned to the so-called *Compañía de Depósito* (Storage Company). All the tanks in this batch, except the command tanks, belonged to the *Ausf. A* variant, called "Krupp" in Spain because of their power plant.

The second batch of German tanks arrived in Spain by late November 1936—twenty-one *Panzer I*s, probably of the *Ausf. B* variant. Fifteen of them, plus a command tank, were used to establish the third company of the Nationalist *Batallón de Carros de Combate* in December. A further five were kept as reserves to make up losses. Finally, the *Legión Cóndor* accounts recorded a third batch of ten *Panzerkampfwagen I* tanks, although both the delivery date and the tank variant supplied remain unknown. We dare say the arrival date may have been early 1937, to make up the losses so far recorded.

Summing up, these were the seventy-two tanks sent to Spain through the *Legión Cóndor*.

The intense battlefield use, the logical wear of a delicate materiel—almost experimental—and the losses experienced in the hard Spanish conflict made these seventy-two tanks insufficient to maintain the battalion operational, so the Spanish military authorities decided to ask Germany for a larger number of panzers "if possible with a 20-mm or larger gun," to face up an enemy that was much superior on the battlefield, the Soviet T-26.

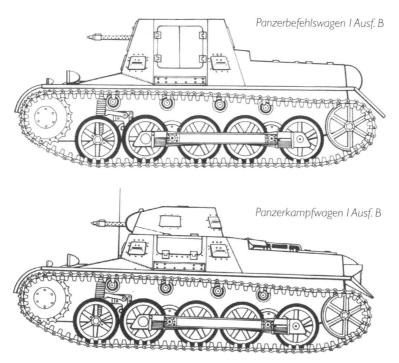

Panzerbefehlswagen I Ausf. B

Panzerkampfwagen I Ausf. B

The German tanks, although widely outclassed by the Soviet tanks, were used with the efficient German doctrine of the time and afforded good results to the Nationalists, who were conscious of their serious shortcomings. (J.M. Campesino via Raúl Arias)

The corresponding requests were transmitted through the Spanish-German HISMA Ltda. company, the first one on 13 July 1937 and the second one on 12 November 1938.

The first request was transmitted by the Generalissimo's HQs, which asked *General Sander* (Hugo Sperrle) to try and speed up the delivery of the thirty tanks ordered in Berlin, as well as additional materiel including fifty 3.7-cm *Pak 35/36*. The mediation of the head of the *Legión Cóndor* must have been decisive, as eighteen *Panzerkampfwagen I Ausf. A* tanks arrived by sea at the Arsenal at El Ferrol on an unrecorded German ship on 25 August. Five days later, on 30 August, the other twelve tanks, up to the thirty requested, arrived in Seville.

The Germans trained the first Spanish crews in a short time. On 1 November 1936 they were already fighting on the Madrid front. (J.M. Campesino via Raúl Arias)

All of them were sent to Cubas de la Sagra, where a 16-tank company was established. The rest were kept as reserves to fulfil the needs of the companies to make up combat losses.

The second request, transmitted through *Maj* Wilhelmi, the German liaison officer between *Gruppe Imker* and the Generalissimo HQs, asked for *"20 German tanks, some of them armed with 20-mm gun or larger calibre."*

That request got a positive answer, and the twenty tanks ordered were delivered to the *Agrupación de Carros de Combate* by *"negrillo"* personnel, on 20 January 1939. All of them were of the Krupp-powered *Panzer I Ausf A* model. This armor materiel completed the total supplies that the Germans sent to Spain during the Civil War. They were a total of 122 *Panzerkampfwagen Is* of the A, B, and command (*Panzerbefehlwagen*) variants, a figure that can be broken up as follows:

The *Panzerbefehlswagen I Ausf. Bs* that arrived in Spain were quite a different version from those that became known during the invasion of Poland, on 1 September 1939. They lacked the built over fixed turret and had vision slits for the tank commander. The position of the machine gun also lacked the ball socket that characterized this tank later. In this picture the St Andrew's Cross arms on a white field for air identification are very conspicuous. (via Oscar Bruña)

- 4 *Panzerbefehlswagen I Ausf. Bs*
- 21 *Panzerkampfwagen I Ausf. Bs*
- 96 *Panzerkampfwagen I Ausf. As*
- 1 *Panzerkampfwagen I Ausf. As* (*ohne aufbau*).

Note: there may have been small variations in this distribution established by the authors and backed by several empirical and theoretical verifications of the tanks present in Spain, although not supported by any contemporary official document.

By early 1937, the light weight of these tanks and the lack of fire power to confront their Russian adversaries, fitted with a powerful 45-mm gun, urged the Nationalist command to start a study to fit 20-mm guns on Italian (Fiat-Ansaldo CV-33/35) and German (*Panzer I Ausf A*) tanks. After fitting Italian Breda 20-mm machine-guns to both tank types, it was concluded that the German tank achieved the best performances, and the modification of one tank for each of the existing sections was ordered. Thus, it was intended to improve the offensive capacity of the Nationalist armored units, clearly outnumbered and outclassed by their Republican opponents.

A *Panzerbefehlswagen I Ausf.B* covered in snow during the offensive on Teruel in January 1938. That was one of the hardest winters of the time, with temperatures nearing -20° C. Even so, the German tanks did work. (Authors)

The poor fire rate of the "*negrillo*" tanks made the Nationalist authorities look for a conversion, fitting them with an Italian 20-mm Breda machine gun, and different changes to the turret. (J.M. Campesino via Raúl Arias)

Top and next page: two of the rare surviving graphic evidence examples of the existence of the four *Panzer I Ausf. A* tanks with a 20-mm Breda gun. They had a dull life in the units, and the Germans of the *Drohne* did not like the conversion at all. In Germany, the 20-mm gun-armed *Panzer II* was already available. (Authors)

(via J. Mazarrasa)

A total of four *Panzer I Ausf As* were thus modified, although the capture and phase-in of a certain amount of Soviet T-26Bs made the conversion unnecessary.

In any case, Colonel von Thoma and his men did not like the idea at all, and even called the tanks thus modified "death tanks" for, in their opinion, the holes pierced in the armor for the aiming of the main weapon were an invitation for the enemy to kill the gunner. It was through *Maj* Wilhelmi, the abovementioned liaison officer of the German Military mission at the Generalissimo's HQs, that he asked to put an end to the conversion of a further six tanks that *general* García Pallasar—Commanding General of Artillery at the C.G.G.—had ordered *teniente coronel* Pujales to deliver by late 1937. It was stopped at once, and no further tanks were modified, which subsequently upset *general* García Pallasar, who sent an official telegram dated 15 January 1938 telling the *3ª Sección del Estado Mayor del Generalísimo*:

> ". . . that the only way of avoiding the defect remarked is to cover the small slot pierced on the armour for the aiming with rifle bullet-proof glass (...) It is our opinion, given this difficulty, that it must be Your Excellency's choice to decide what is better, either to go without the possibility of fighting the enemy tanks with others able to pierce them, or to let Colonel von THOMA's soldiers run the risk of dying inside the tanks because a rifle bullet might get in through a small window which, on the other hand, must and can be kept closed till the moment of aiming.
> . . ."

Gruppe Thoma supplied the tank unit with an anti-tank gun company for combined operations for support against enemy tanks. That company was made up of eight anti-tank guns, called 3.7-cm *Panzerabwehrkanone (Pak) 35/36*, all of them towed by off-road tractor trucks, Krupp L-2H43 Protze; and a further five guns for independent operations, which were carried on trucks.

A war scene with a German 3.7-cm Pak 35/36 anti-tank gun. (J.M. Campesino via Raúl Arias)

Above left: A 45-mm anti-tank gun of Soviet origin (although of German inspiration and patent). Nationalist captures augmented the anti-tank armament of the *Agrupación de Cañones Antitanques* (anti-tank guns nationalist unit). (J.M. Campesino via Raúl Arias) Above right: A member of *Panzer Gruppe Drohne* talks to an old lady during the campaign in the North. Behind, several Krupp Protze light trucks.

Apart form this company, which made part of the tank unit, Germany sent nearly 300 guns of the same type and caliber to Spain in several shipments, which were used to establish powerful *Agrupación de Cañones Antitanque* (Anti-tank Gun Groups) under the command of *comandante* José del Toro that operated on the different fronts during the whole war, including, apart from the German materiel, Russian 45/44-mm guns and other types, all of them captured from the Republicans.

Gruppe Drohne organized the training of the Spanish officers, NCOs, and troops of the arm, and the commander of the anti-tank instructors contingent was *Maj* Peter Jansa, who was in command from November 1936 to 18 March 1938, when he returned to Germany.

Panzerabwehrkanone 35/36 de 3.7 cm

A member of *Panzer Gruppe Drohne* training on the 7.92-mm Dreyse machine gun on tripod. The *Heer* supplied the contingent in Spain with 438 machine guns of this type and 200 tripods. Out of these 438 machine guns, 238 were on the 122 tanks on Spanish soil during the war (one each for the four *Panzerbefehlswagen I Ausf. B* command tanks and 234 for the 117 *Panzerkampfwagen I Ausf. A* and *B* tanks, each fitted with two. The tank driver training types, called by the Germans "*ohne Aufbau*," had no armament). The other 200 were arms like the one in the picture, fitted with a tripod. (Authors)

4

Von Thoma and the Nationalist Military Authorities

Oberstleutnant Wilhelm von Thoma, commander of the German *Heer* instructors contingent in Spain, was appointed Tank Inspector by Generalissimo Franco, a nominal post with wide real functions on training, tactical use, and doctrine of an arm that was booming in Germany, although in Spain, despite its use in some operations of the Moroccan campaigns, had not been properly developed and had not attracted enough attention after their end back in 1926.

Two facts were fundamental at the time of making the decision. On the one hand, there was von Thoma's role in the development of a modern powerful armored force in Germany since the 1920s—along with his compatriots von Lutz and Guderian. On the other hand, the fact that most of the armored equipment sent to the Nationalists was of German origin, as well as all of the instructors.

Left, the teniente *coronel* Díaz de la Lastra, commander of *Agrupación de Carros de Combate de la Legión*. Right is *Oberstleutnant* Wilhelm Ritter von Thoma. (Madrid, 1939). (Manuel Álvaro via Raúl Arias)

From an organizational point of view, Wilhelm *Ritter* von Thoma was dependent on *Oberstleutnant* von Funck, Military Attaché in Burgos, Chief of the German Army mission at the Generalissimo's HQs and responsible for the whole *Heer* detachment in Spain, the so-called *Gruppe Imker*.

Von Thoma's relationships with the Nationalist military authorities were usually cordial so to speak, although the character of the German commander and the circumstances of the conflict itself contributed to some tension at times in an obvious manner. One of them took place on 29 April 1938, when von Thoma sent a thorough report on the tanks, their use and training, a report where he unambiguously spoke his mind without trying to be diplomatic; he unveiled the reality and revealed the serious structural lacks of the armored unit of the Nationalist Army.

The second, racial controversy between the *Oberstleutnant* and the Nationalist authorities was maybe more serious, and here the German brought up some Teutonic arrogance, bordering on conceit. The notice on the *Boletín Oficial del Estado* (Spanish official gazette) on the course for prospective tank crews, apparently without the previous communiqué to the then "Tank Inspector" von Thoma came eight months later, and on this occasion the German got involved in a dry epistolary controversy with the successor of *general* Orgaz in command of the *Jefatura de M.I.R.*, Infantry *coronel* Ricardo Fernández de Tamarit. This ended up in a most wanted stalemate thanks to the flair of the Spanish soldier who knew how to deal with people.

The Controversial "von Thoma" Report

By late April, Colonel von Thoma wrote a report for *Maj* Wilhelmi—liaison officer in von Funck's team—so that he delivered it at the Generalissimo's HQs, where he was posted. In that report, von Thoma was very critical of the way in which the recruitment and training of the tank crews was being carried out, mainly since the establishment of the *Bandera de Carros de Combate de la Legión* for, from that moment on, the figures of candidates for the tank crews were severely reduced, restricting them to the corps itself, with the serious question that, on some occasions, the *banderas* chose personnel for training not according to their suitability, but rather in order to "get rid" of him.

Oberstleutnant Ritter von Thoma, issuing orders to a Spanish tank officer. Behind, wearing a peaked cap and a long beard, *Hauptman* Adolf Clauss, the interpreter of the German colonel during the entire Spanish Civil War. (J.M. Campesino via Raúl Arias)

Because of its importance and interest, some excerpts are quoted here that show both the character and the mood of the commander of the German *Panzer Gruppe* by that time, as well as his obvious involvement in the training of the Spanish tank crews, which, in our opinion and beyond malicious interpretations, honors him and proves the zeal of the German officer at work.

Report on the Tank Corps.

Based on my thorough observation on the fronts and at the Tank Training School at Cubas, and in order to achieve a better use of the arm, I beg your permission to say what follows:

The current condition of the tanks, both as regards the personnel and their training is honestly poor. In such condition, this corps cannot possibly attain the performance the High Command has the right to expect from it.

The cause of the problem lies in the current organization that can be easily perfected, and visible improvements could be accomplished in a few weeks.

Before the Tank Corps was transferred to the *Legión*, there was a larger amount of personnel for selection, as there were a number of volunteers' applications. At that time, little attention was being paid to the need to select personnel either, for training was being carried out in haste because of the requirements of the campaign and the tank driver should have got at least the basic technical knowledge. Despite the intelligence and ease to understand of the Spanish soldier, it is not possible to train tank drivers that are able to solve technical problems on the front if they have not had the previous experience of a trade of this sort. Soldiers of this class need several months' training. The question of the tank gunners is an easier one to solve, although they certainly must learn the practice of firing with the optical equipment from within the tank.

As the Tank Corps joined the *Legión*, the replacement personnel available has been considerably reduced and it must be stated that this personnel does not always meet the conditions expected from a soldier of the Tank Arm, because quite often there is personnel that is posted here that the *Bandera* does not want for any reasons whatsoever, without an application by the man in question and without the previous knowledge that is needed for tank driving. It entirely looks as though it has become a punishment posting. Nothing can be expected from a troop in these conditions, without technical or tactical training.

This is my proposal: at the Tank Training School, established on His Excellence the Generalissimo's request at Cubas, there must be permanently posted at least 50 volunteer soldiers, i.e., 25 drivers and 25 gunners, who after a 4-week training will be posted to the front as replacements as soon as they are needed. These figures must be immediately filled in with suitable personnel. The group CO is always in charge of making sure there are volunteer personnel previously tested for suitability for the Tank Arm. A corps like this, with so difficult requests, has to be bad without volunteers.

The Reds' *Boletín Oficial del Estado*, regarding the War Minister in Valencia, no. 108 of 5 May 1937 shows the orders favorable for their tank volunteers. (...)

(...) The group CO and the company COs must always stay by their companies, even on combat duties. Constant presence is quite often difficult because companies operate too far apart from each other, so the group CO must stay with the company whose tactical operation is more difficult. **These separate interventions make supplies operations difficult, as there is only one mobile workshop available** and the knowledge of the personnel for small front repairs is so poor because the personnel is not properly instructed and thus many times tanks have had to be carried to the workshops hundreds of kilometres away. The same applies to the personnel for the Russian tanks, who need different training, and the anti-tank guns attached to the tank group that, for the lack of training, cannot show positive results.

The transport company is so scattered that it is impossible to direct them (...)

(...) The group CO and the company COs must stay by their troops in order to keep an eye on them, and not anywhere else in the rearguard, far away from their units. (...)

(...) Tank training has to be carried out like at the other academies, calmly, separately and following a prearranged syllabus. Showing the soldiers the tanks for a few hours is no training at all but self-deception that is to be paid dear on the front. Despite my constant demands, I have not managed to get personnel for tank training. Some of them, of little use, who have been discharged, have been at Cubas for a short time and these are four drivers and gunners for the light tanks and four for the Russian tanks. **For that reason, the tank group can never make up casualties with trained personnel and has become more and more tactically and technically deficient.**

Unlike the tank group, I can say that the training of *comandante* Toro's anti-tank companies is in very good condition, and the personnel posted for training arrives in time, so casualties can be made up with thoroughly trained personnel (...)

Burgos, 29 April 1938. II Triumphant Year.[13]"

(Authors' **bold** words)

Al portador de este carnet

Sr. D. Guillermo v. Thoma

Coronel

se autoriza libre circulación por todo el territorio ocupado por el Ejército Nacional. Se ruega a todas las autoridades civiles y Militares le presten toda clase de facilidades, manifestándose al mismo tiempo que dicho señor está autorizado a llevar armas.

Spanish military card under the name of *coronel* Guillermo v. Thoma, belonging to the tank "Section." (Manuel Álvaro)

Von Thoma's harshness in the report is extraordinary, and certainly his discrediting views of the changes at the Tank Battalion and its transfer to the *Legión* are the most striking, although the whole shows harsh criticism of the overall operation of the tank unit, entirely in Nationalist hands, including the Transport Company, the Workshop, and the Tank Training School. And it is precisely the latter that attracts the core of his criticism, or at least the hardest part of it. Von Thoma also complained about the disbandment of the tank units, all of them operating at places too far apart from each other, which caused real logistic problems for the Workshop and the Transport Company. To be remarked are the good words he addressed to the gunners of the 3.7-cm Pak anti-tank guns under *comandante* José del Toro's orders, for whom he spared no praise for their good training of the prospective gunners, always using laconic German military vocabulary.

Obersteutnant von Thoma standing next to his interpreter, Adolf Clauss. The latter had fought on the Guadarrama front since August 1936, in the Falange from Valladolid. With the arrival of *Ritter* von Thoma he became an interpreter until the end of the war. His work was tarnished by some misunderstandings with the German tank Inspector and with Infantry *coronel* Ricardo Fernández Tamarit, interim CO of the M.I.R. (J.M. Campesino via Raúl Arias)

The von Thoma-Tamarit Affair

Eight months after the report, a notice was published in the *Boletín Oficial del Estado* nº 183 dated 31 December 1938 for the selection of candidates for a tank-training course at the school established at Casarrubuelos. This notice originated from a request by the *teniente coronel* commanding the *Agrupación de Carros de Combate*, Gonzalo Díaz de la Lastra, to the *M.I.R.* HQs Office on the 20th of that month, for the proposal of a tank training course for a career or an empowered major, three captains (career, temporary, or empowered), and twelve junior officers, all of them from the Infantry.

Thirteen days later, von Thoma sent a telegram to the Staff at Cubas de la Sagra from Saragossa, addressed to Infantry *coronel* Ricardo Fernández de Tamarit, temporary CO of the *M.I.R.* The telegram said:

> "On the 31 December *Boletín Oficial* Number 183 there is a notice for a tank training course.
>
> Do please pretty clearly explain to Tamarit that I must be reported beforehand as regards the plans, for that is requested according to the Spanish provisions on the Tank Inspector. Otherwise, I shall stop my contribution and that of the instructor personnel, who is dependent on myself solely and no one else.
>
> Given the current circumstances, I think that a 60-day course is utterly insufficient, with just 30-day theoretical training. I beg Tamarit to give me detailed explanations on all this and, once he has done it, I shall decide whether the German instructors should contribute. On that regard, I have addressed *teniente coronel* Lastra and the Chief of my team at Cubas.

Spanish and German soldiers of von Thoma. (J.M. Campesino via Raúl Arias)

On the Generalissimo's orders, I have been appointed Tank Inspector and I demand to be heard beforehand. Otherwise, I shall complain.

The telegram shall be sent to Tamarit in Spanish.

                                                    Thoma."

It is obvious, after reading the telegram, that the "Tank Inspector," Colonel Wilhelm von Thoma, was really upset. If he was in a bad mood, this was the result of lack of style by the Spaniards—say discourtesy—as he was overlooked in questions as important as the training of the prospective tank units of the Nationalist Army.

The answer from *coronel* Tamarit—an upright, serious, and efficient man—did not take long, and on 17 January, after reporting—according to the rules in these cases—to the Generalissimo's HQs, he sent a very long letter to the German, in precise, clear, and forceful language, although showing restraint, good manners, and diplomacy, to explain to von Thoma his absolute disagreement with the statements in the latter's telegram.

In the first place, according to Tamarit, Chief of the *Agrupación de Carros de Combate*, *teniente coronel* de la Lastra, had asked the HQs' Office of the *M.I.R.* that a tank command and use course be given every month at the school at Casarrubuelos, and once finished, all those taking part be attached to the *Agrupación* for another month for practice, after which they should rejoin the original corps waiting for a vacancy at the *Agrupación*.

In a conversation Tamarit himself had with von Thoma on 20 December 1938 through the German interpreter Capt Adolfo Clauss Kindt, apart from other subjects such as machine gun courses, at San Roque, Cadiz, or signals, at Monasterio de Rodilla, Burgos, the tank courses subject was dealt with, and it was decided to present *teniente coronel* Díez de la Lastra's proposal to the H.E. Generalissimo, with the remark that von Thoma agreed and would contribute with his collaboration and assistance.

Tamarit stressed—in order to reinforce his position—that the whole matter had been reported in written form (record number 86,220) to hotel "María Isabel" in Burgos, addressed to Capt Clauss as usual. What is more, Tamarit stated in his reply that the conditions for the course and duration of the same fitted in with the verbal agreement with the German in the interview through the interpreter Capt Clauss.

Translation problems? An oversight in the delivery of documents? Misinterpretations?

The truth is that von Thoma must have been really upset so as to threaten with the withdrawal of his subordinates in training tasks, and Tamarit, as it can be seen at the end of his letter, must have felt really sad for the arrogance in the German's telegram.

After an exhaustive and detailed review of the development of the events surrounding the tank-training course in question, *coronel* Ricardo Fernández Tamarit ended with the following plea:

"...Y.L. was listened to previously and your indications attended to with my uttermost zeal, care and respect during my temporary employment, and I have tried to attend whatever I was asked on Y.L.'s behalf, solving immediately what was in my powers and asking the Superiors with all urgency for what was not included.

Mr Klauss (sic, Capt Clauss actually) is perfectly aware of this, (...)

(...) No respect, attention and consideration that Y.L., your person and your representation deserve have been spared. It is thus not necessary to remind me of precepts that I have not forgotten nor is the use of the statements that you will stop your valuable collaboration and that of your instructors; that once my explanations have been heard you will decide whether the German instructors will contribute and you demand to be listened to before because, otherwise, you shall complain.(...)

(...) I take the liberty to add, Y.L., with all my respect and consideration, that I would have better liked you to have refrained from using phrases of coercive concept by reminding you who you are addressing, because I never omit the considerations that are due to others, and have acquired, for that only fact, the indisputable right of reciprocity in the procedure. Mr Klaus (sic), no matter how respectable he may be, is after all a subordinate element and earnestly I dare beg Y.L., when you address me through him, to try to avoid the phrases addressed at me, not justified by my conduct, neither suitable for what my age and my efforts –if there is no other reason– give me a right to expect. (...)

(...) I hope with confidence in Y.L.'s rectitude that you will render me justice and will admit that I have not dispensed with anything that should not be omitted.

Let God protect Spain and Y.L. for many years
Burgos, 17 January 1939
III Triumphant Year
TEMPORARY CHIEF COLONEL"

The incident was solved after a meeting of both colonels. *Oberstleutnant* Wilhelm *Ritter* von Thoma obviously did not stop his collaboration in trai, nor changed anything until the end of the war. The course for tank officers at the Casarrubuelos School was carried out normally, with a 30-day theoretical training and 30-day practice duration, at the *Agrupación*.

5

Gruppe Drohne Special Training

The *Gruppe Drohne* instructors not only showed the Spaniards the use of panzers (driving, technique, tactics...), but also put a lot of effort into training the Spaniards in other matters, maybe not so eye-catching but equally fundamental and important in the framework of modern multidisciplinary warfare.

Special training carried out by the *Gruppe* spanned such different aspects as the use of and practice with flame throwers, anti-tank guns, or Italian 47 mm anti-tank guns; special vehicle driving courses, such as the heavy trucks of the transport company and light Protze tractors for anti-tank guns; and courses for armorer masters, engine repairs... A detailed review of the most important ones comes next.

The most numerous German guns in the Spanish conflict were the 3.7-cm Pak 35/36, like the one in the picture. Most were handed over to the Spanish. (Authors)

The 37-mm Anti-Tank Gun Training Group

Twenty-four 3.7-cm Pak 35/36 anti-tank guns and a group of instructors under the orders of *Hauptm* Peter Jansa arrived in Spain along with the first two *Panzerkampfwagen I Ausf. A* tank companies.

The 3.7-cm gun was developed by Rheinmetall-Borsig in 1933. From then on, it became very popular and a real success, and was thus adopted by several countries, such as Italy, Holland, Japan, the USA, and the Soviet Union. Although at the start of the Second World War this gun was obsolete and practically inefficient, in Spain it was perfectly suitable to fight the tanks it had to face.

Thirteen of these twenty-four first guns that arrived in Seville, as well as the rest of the *Gruppe Thoma* equipment, were used to establish the so-called *Compañia Motorizada de Cañones Anticar* (Anti-tank Gun Motorized Company) that was attached to the German armored group from the start, and then to the tank battalion and its successors.

Eight of the thirteen 3.7-cm guns of the company had a similar number of off-road Krupp L-2H43 Protze light trucks, adapted as tractors. The other five anti-tank guns of the same model were set aside to operate independently from the tank unit, e.g. as support for Infantry columns, or to give cover in river crossings, etc., and were thus not towed by off-road tractors, but had to be loaded on trucks that were strong enough for the task. These first five Pak guns were the embryos of the so-called *Agrupación de Cañones Anticarro de 37 mm* that had over 300 Pak guns during the war that arrived from Germany in different batches.

A good picture of the German 3.7-cm *Panzerabwehrkanone* (Pak) anti-tank guns. The tank unit established by the Germans had thirteen of these guns in a company. Besides, the Nationalist Army got quite a large number of these guns with which the *Agrupación de Cañones Antitanques de 37 mm* was established during the conflict.

Several *Gruppe Drohne* anti-tank guns hitched to the Kupp Protze tractor-trucks. Notice the good camouflage of the guns and vehicles. (Authors)

Just like the tanks, the anti-tank guns were sent by rail from Seville to Las Herguijuelas castle, Cáceres, for training and incoporation. In fact, the chief instructor, *Hauptm* Jansa, and his men started the training of the first Spanish crews by mid-October, when artillery *alférez* Pedro Sanz Ruano was sent to Cáceres to take command of the unit on the Generalissimo's order to the chief general of the *Ejército del Norte* (North Army), as well as a warrant officer, five sergeants, eleven corporals, sixty gunners, twelve drivers, a carpenter, a mechanic, a mason, two clerks, and eight soldiers. These were the Spanish men of the first anti-tank unit established by the Artillery Corps in the Nationalist area.

Apart from the abovementioned German CO Peter Jansa, 2/Lts Gerhard Nethe, Karl Rieschick, and Johann Vermeulen, as well as W/Os Hans Novak, Martin Wolf, Hugo Ullrich, and Johann Seifert were also part of the anti-tank training unit, in addition to interpreter Josef Wieseler.

One month later, on 16 November, a new training period was announced. New equipment was about to come from Germany—both tanks and anti-tank guns—and there were plans to establish a third *Panzer I* company with them—to be attached to the two already fighting in the columns marching on Madrid—and three new anti-tank companies.

By late November thirty-two new 3.7-cm Pak guns and ten Krupp Protze light trucks arrived, and three anti-tank companies, with ten guns each, two of them on trucks, and a motorized one with the Protzes, were established.

In total, seven officers (including a captain), thirty warrant officers, one hundred and twenty gunners, and ten drivers were trained, and the duration of the course—which started by mid-December—was fifteen days. Each company had ten guns, two of which were left at Cubas as reserves.

The first of the companies established and trained was commanded by Infantry *capitán* José del Toro— the prospective CO of the *Agrupación Española de Cañones Antitanque—* and was attached to the columns marching on Madrid, as replacements of the first guns sent before, sincee the latter were badly in need of repairs.

The successive deliveries of anti-tank equipment made *Hauptm* Jansa's group very busy during the whole war, a work that continued even after Jansa had returned to Germany on 18 March 1938.

In October that same year, Colonel von Thoma proposed to the Generalissimo's HQs the establishment of an *Escuela de Anticarros* attached to the HQs themselves, within the frame of a more ambitious project called "*Centro de Instrucción y Reserva de Carros y Anticarros*" (Training and Reserve Anti-tank Gun Center).

Teniente coronel Martinez Simancas— a competent field officer posted as Secretary of the *2ª Sección de la Jefatura de M.I.R.*—was given a very detailed project of the Tank School in Germany as a model for Spain, during his visit to that country in 1938.

The first anti-tank gun training courses took place in Cáceres, although they were later given at Cubas de la Sagra, and later on moved to the villages of Carranque and Cedillo del Condado.

Although some 3.7-cm Pak 35/36 anti-tank gun batteries had light trucks to be used as tractors, for which reason they could be classified as motorized, most of them had to be loaded on trucks, and the procedure is shown in the left picture. In the same way, the rest of the transport manoeuvres to the gun emplacement were carried out by hand, as seen in the right picture. (Authors)

Flamethrower training

Maj Peter Jansa, the anti-tank gun chief instructor, had also been in charge of flamethrowers training since January 1937.

A widely used weapon during the First World War, a flamethrower, as the name suggests, was just a device that could throw a flammable liquid at a certain distance, under pressure, producing ignition as the liquid came out of the tank through a hose long enough to prevent burning the operator himself.

(J.M. Campesino via Raúl Arias)

Top and Above left: *Panzerkampfwagen I Ausf A* fitted with a small flamethrower device, and used by the tank companies at Talavera. (Authors) Above right: Training at Oropesa, Toledo, on the light flamethrowers supplied by *Gruppe Thoma* in October 1936. (Authors)

(Authors)

Assembly and training tasks with a large flamethrower, also called "trench type." The five supplied by *Gruppe Thoma* in October 1936 were mounted on armored trucks.

(J.M. Campesino via Raúl Arias)

A total of nine flamethrowers, four of the light model called *Flammenwerfer* 35 and five of the heavy model, also called "large" or "trench" type, were supplied through *Gruppe Thoma*. As early as 17 October 1936, the *C.G.G.* sent a telegram to *general* Varela telling "... with the utmost urgency, make the arrangements so that an officer and thirty soldiers chosen among the *Banderas* from those columns (...) are sent to Cáceres to be dispatched to Arguijuela (sic) castle where they will be trained in the use of flame throwers. Training timetables shall be established at the castle by Mr Thoma. Once the training is finished, they will join their units to operate these devices..."

At the end, no training was given at Las Herguijuelas castle, but at Oropesa, Toledo, and nine days later, the *Tercio* men joined the front at Talavera with their brand new flamethrowers.

Out of the four light devices, with 25-30 m effective range, 10-sec fire duration and a tank capacity of 11.8 litres of flammable liquid, two were supplied to *general* Varela on 24 October; one was fitted to a *Panzerkampfwagen I Ausf A tank*, and left on 27 October at 09.00 hrs with the rest of the tanks of the two companies and the anti-tank guns, destination Talavera. The rest were left at Las Herguijuelas castle for training.

Regarding the five devices of the heavy type, also called "large" or "trench" type, three of them were sent to the Talavera front on 26 October, on some armored trucks that were hastily supplied, with different faults that were repaired at the "*negrillo*" workshops in a short time. The other two were left for the meantime at Las Herguijuelas castle for training.

A few days later, on 1 November, Varela was ordered to name fifteen men for training in the use of the three flamethrowers left at Las Herguijuelas, "...Training preferably to be given where Mr Thomas (sic) is..." The two large ones were to be fitted to tanks, the conversion being carried out at Quismondo where the "*negrillos*" had established their workshops.

After several deliveries of German equipment acquired through HISMA Ltda., the *Tercio* established a flamethrower company with three sections, two light and one heavy, each of them with nine flamethrowers (which made a total of eighteen light and nine heavy devices). Besides, at Cubas de la Sagra, von Thoma had a further twenty-five light and twenty heavy devices, ready to be assigned to a likely second flamethrower company that never materialized. Their use was quite reduced during the Civil War, and their main missions were more similar to those of the units of the Chemical Warfare Service, to decontaminate areas that had become impregnated, as well as fighting enemy tanks.

Four snapshots of the *Flammenpanzer I Ausf.A.*, tested in Spain in October 1936, just after the establishment of *Gruppe Thoma*. (Authors)

Excellent picture showing one of the huge Vomag DL-48 trucks with an Sd.Ah 115 tank carrier platform and two *Panzerkampfwagen I Ausf.As*. (J.M. Campesino via Raúl Arias)

Special equipment training

Apart from the panzers, Pak guns, and *Flammenwerfer*, the *Heer* contingent travelled to Spain with numerous and varied equipment, all of which was a novelty for the Spanish soldiers, and for which it was necessary to organize training classes.

–Tank transportation on heavy vehicles

The German transport company— commanded by *Oblt* Hans Schruefer for the whole war—was in charge of organizing and training a Spanish company for that purpose, training an officer and seventy-five heavy truck drivers in the basic tasks carried out by that unit, such as driving, maintenance of transportation equipment, general mechanics (engine, signals, etc.), armored equipment stowage, unit organization et al.

–Krupp L-H43 Protze *Kfz* 69 light truck drivers

The vehicles chosen to tow the motorized companies' Pak guns, as we have seen in a previous chapter, were the Krupp L-2H43 Protze Kfz 69 light trucks, for whose training and driving several courses for the members of the motorized companies were given, both for that assigned to the *Batallón de Carros de Combate* and those belonging to *comandante* del Toro's *Agrupación de Cañones Antitanque*. In total about thirty drivers were trained, a similar number to the Protze trucks that arrived with *Gruppe Thoma*.

–Workshop personnel

The *Gruppe Thoma* company workshop, commanded by *Obleutnant* Albert Schneider for the whole war, trained a group of workshop masters, assistants, and mechanics—both engine and armament—of around eighty Spaniards, who joined the workshop unit and the mobile workshops of the Nationalist *Batallón de Carros de Combate*.

Top: a Krupp Protze moving across a watercourse. (Canario Azaola) Bottom: a *Drohne* Workshop instructor, at Cubas, teaching an aspiring armorer one of the Dreyse machine guns of a *Panzer I Ausf. A.* (Authors)

The traces of hard combat are evident on the armor of this *Panzerkampfwagen I Ausf.* A tank captured by the Republicans who, most probably, were not able to repair it. (National Library)

6

The Members of *Gruppe Drohne*

Name lists of *Gruppe Thoma* personnel as per units
DROHNE TANK GROUP, COMPANY AND SECTION COs

NAME	RANK	JOINED	LEFT	REMARKS
Von Thoma, Wilhelm	Col	23/09/36	31/05/39	*Gruppe Drohne* CO
Bothe, Karl-Ernst	Maj	01/11/36	16/12/37	
Crohn, Herbert	Maj	01/11/37	31/05/39	
Wolf, Heinz	Maj	08/10/36	25/07/37	01/05/37 became Academy Chief
Ziegler, Joachim	Maj	08/10/36	18/03/38	01/05/37 became Academy Chief
Von der Planitz, Ferdinand	Capt	08/10/36	28/09/37	
Trippe, Gustav	Capt	01/03/38	31/05/39	KIA (Fatarella) 14-11-38
Willing, Gerhard	Capt	08/10/36	14/09/37	
Von Falkenberg, Hans-Joachim	Lt	01/11/37	02/05/38	
Fremm, Ernst	Lt	01/11/37	31/05/39	
Von Levetzow, Axel	Lt	01/11/37	31/05/39	
Von Moerner, Hannibal	Lt	08/10/36	24/07/37	KIA (Brunete) 24-07-37
Pfannkuche, Karl	Lt	01/11/36	06/12/37	
Von Pilsach, Ottfried S.	Lt	08/10/36	15/10/37	
Strauchmann, Erwin	Lt	08/10/36	20/07/37	

Above: In a Wanderer light car, the CO of the 2. Tank Company, the then *Oberleutnant* Heinz Wolf, interpreter Karl Kuebler and, in the rear, the company deputy chief, *Oberleutnant* Gerhard Willing. (J.M. Campesino via Raúl Arias)

Left: Left to right, *Leutnant* Hannibal von Moerner, *Dolmetscher* Albert Barthels (interpreter of the 2. Company) and *Oberleutnant* Heinz Wolf, the company CO. (J.M. Campesino via Raúl Arias)

TANK INSTRUCTOR 2/LTs

NAME	JOINED	LEFT	REMARKS
Adolph, Gerhard	08/10/36	01/07/37	
Boche, Gerhard	08/10/36	31/05/39	01/05/37 moved to *Academia de Infantería*
Busch, Albert	08/10/36	21/10/37	
Dziadek, Fritz	08/10/36	09/08/37	
Haase, Friedrich	08/10/36	03/10/37	01/06/37 moved to workshops
Hoppe, Wolf Horst	01/03/38	31/05/39	
Kambach, Wilhelm	08/10/36	09/08/37	
Keddig, Rudolf	08/10/36	01/07/37	
Kempe, Richard	08/10/36	15/12/36	
Lindner, Richard	01/11/36	09/08/37	
Maeder, Otto	08/10/36	01/04/37	
Melzer, Günther	08/10/36	15/11/37	01/05/37 moved to *Academia de Infantería*
Meyerhofer, Hans	08/10/36	13/05/37	01/05/37 moved to *Academia de Infantería*
Paul, Rolf	08/10/36	03/10/37	
Poppelreuther, Heinrich	01/11/36	09/08/37	
Roggenbach, Joachim	08/10/36	15/11/37	
Rust, Rudolf	08/10/36	31/05/39	01/06/37 joined Staff
Schmidt, Bruno	08/10/36	31/05/39	01/06/37 moved to *Academia de Infantería*
Schulz, Hermann	08/10/36	01/12/37	01/05/37 moved to *Academia de Infantería*
Wacker, Friedrich	01/09/37	31/05/39	
Weiss, Karl	08/10/36	29/10/36	
Wolter, Artur	08/10/36	16/03/37	

INTERPRETERS ASSIGNED TO TANK UNITS

NAME	JOINED	LEFT	REMARKS
Barthels, Albert	15/11/36	28/09/37	Front service
Bebber, Wilhelm	01/11/36	31/05/39	01/05/37 moved to *Academia de Infantería*
Drechsel, Max	01/11/36	31/05/39	Front service
Kuebler, Karl	23/09/36	31/05/39	Front service
Vietsch, Hermann	08/10/36	31/05/39	01/05/37 moved to *Academia de Infantería*
Winkler, Heinrich	08/10/36	31/05/39	Front service

Left: The German volunteers of the *Panzer-Gruppe Thoma* make a stop in front of the Ávila wall. (J.M. Campesino via Raúl Arias)

Right: *Panzer Gruppe Drohne* volunteer. (J.M. Campesino via Raúl Arias)

TANK INSTRUCTOR W/Os

NAME	JOINED	LEFT	REMARKS
Abraham, Kurt	08/10/36	15/11/37	
Adomat, Walter	08/10/36	16/12/37	
Alter, Ernst	08/10/36	21/07/37	01/05/37 moved to *Academia de Infantería*
Arnold, Willi	08/10/36	20/07/37	
Arnold, Oskar	08/10/36	20/07/37	
Badhke, Helmuth	08/10/36	03/10/37	
Balke, Werner	08/10/36	20/03/37	
Bartholomae, Karl	08/10/36	31/05/39	01/05/37 moved to *Academia de Infantería*
Beck, Walter	01/11/36	31/05/39	01/05/37 moved to *Academia de Infantería*
Becker, Heinrich	08/10/36	09/08/37	
Beilfuss, Hans	08/10/36	21/10/37	01/05/37 moved to *Academia de Infantería*
Belewski, Otto	08/10/36	24/07/37	Died of illness 24/07/37 (Cubas)
Beyer, Otto	01/07/37	25/12/37	Instructor on captured Russian tanks
Boelker, Kurt	08/10/36	31/05/39	01/05/37 moved to *Academia de Infantería*
Bolz, Paul	08/10/36	20/12/37	01/05/37 moved to *Academia de Infantería*
Borchers, Heinz	01/10/37	09/04/38	Instructor on captured Russian tanks
Borusiak, Albert	08/10/36	03/10/37	
Bosse, Reinhold	08/10/36	03/10/37	
Brennecke, Walter	01/11/36	21/10/37	
Brinkhus, Otto	08/10/36	03/10/37	
Bussmann, Johannes	08/10/36	03/10/37	
Butz, Adalbert	01/11/36	12/05/37	KIA (Murga) 12/05/37
Cegan, Gerhard	08/10/36	21/07/37	
Cichon, Alois	08/10/36	01/07/37	
Dame, Walter	08/10/36	01/08/37	
Deutsch, Otto	08/10/36	01/07/37	
Dimde, Fritz	08/10/36	07/02/37	
Doering, Helmut	01/06/37	02/05/38	Instructor on captured Russian tanks
Engel, Alfred	08/10/36	15/11/37	01/05/37 moved to *Academia de Infantería*
Ermann, Paul	08/10/36	14/08/37	01/05/37 moved to *Academia de Infantería*
Eysser, Oskar	08/10/36	20/07/37	
Falkenthal, Emil	08/10/36	31/05/39	
Fiedler, Otto	01/10/37	31/05/39	
Freitag, Hans-Joachim	08/10/36	21/10/37	
Friese, Bruno	01/10/37	02/05/38	
Fritsch, Gerhard	08/10/36	29/05/37	
Fude, Erich	08/10/36	03/10/37	01/05/37 moved to *Academia de Infantería*
Gaede, Walter	08/10/36	01/07/37	
Gaertner, Martin	01/04/38	31/05/39	
Geignetter, Willi	01/06/37	09/04/38	
Goetz, Alfred	01/11/36	31/05/39	01/05/37 moved to *Academia de Infantería*
Grapp, Kurt	08/10/36	01/07/37	
Grotephorst, Johann	01/11/36	12/12/37	
Groth, Hans	08/10/36	01/07/37	
Guenther, Erich	08/10/36	03/10/37	
Hagge, Werner	01/09/37	31/05/39	
Hauck, Ernst	08/10/36	01/12/36	
Heidrich, Alfons	01/10/37	02/05/38	
Hill, Franz	08/10/36	20/07/37	
Hobein, August	08/10/36	21/10/37	01/05/37 moved to *Academia de Infantería*
Hoehnow, Helmut	08/10/36	03/10/37	

Hoelk, Klaus	08/10/36	19/07/37	
Hoering, Alfred	08/10/36	11/12/37	
Hoffmann, Jakob	01/06/37	09/02/38	
Hohmeister, Erich	08/10/36	05/11/37	
Horning, Emil	08/10/36	15/11/37	
Huebner, Heinrich	01/11/36	03/10/37	
Huedepohl, Wilhelm	08/10/36	05/04/37	
Jalass, Ernst	08/10/36	15/11/37	01/05/37 moved to *Academia de Infantería*
Joswiak, Franz	01/10/37	31/05/39	
Kannenberg, Kurt	08/10/36	31/05/39	01/05/37 moved to *Academia de Infantería*
Kasimiers, Georg	01/10/37	31/05/39	
Kasulke, Arnold	08/10/36	20/07/37	
Kauermann, Heinz	08/10/36	02/12/37	
Kaufhold, Johann	08/10/36	06/03/37	
Kempe, Paul	08/10/36	09/10/36	Killed in accident (Cáceres)
Keske, Karl	01/06/37	09/04/38	
Kitzing	08/10/36	01/12/37	
Klein, Günther	08/10/36	15/06/37	
Knobloch, Willibald	08/10/36	28/09/37	
Knoski, Fritz	08/10/36	20/07/37	
Kolitz, Erich	01/11/36	26/04/37	
Krajewsky, Heinz	08/10/36	26/02/37	
Kramer, Emil	08/10/36	31/05/39	01/05/37 moved to *Academia de Infantería*
Kruegger, Otto	08/10/36	31/05/39	01/05/37 moved to *Academia de Infantería*
Kucht, Alfred	01/10/37	31/05/39	
Kuhrt, Max	08/10/36	17/09/37	
Kurzweg, Arthur	08/10/36	10/08/37	
Kuschel, Rudolf	08/10/36	31/05/39	01/05/37 moved to *Academia de Infantería*
Lache, Rudolf	08/10/36	15/11/37	
Langhammer, Helmut	08/10/36	21/10/37	Instructor on captured Russian tanks
Lipecky, Siegfried	08/10/36	31/05/39	01/05/37 moved to *Academia de Infantería*
Luethke-Verspohl, Hermann	08/10/36	22/03/37	
Luthe, Ewald	08/10/36	17/08/37	
Machleidt, Alfred	01/11/36	09/04/37	
Makswitak, Otto	08/10/36	01/07/37	
Martin, Gerhard	08/10/36	01/07/37	
Matthews, Alfred	08/10/36	15/11/37	
Mehlis, Walter	08/10/36	01/07/37	
Mels, Willi	08/10/36	20/07/37	
Menzel, Heinz	08/10/36	14/08/37	
Meyer, Wilhelm	08/10/36	16/12/37	01/05/37 moved to *Academia de Infantería*
Muentz, Paul	08/10/36	15/11/37	
Mundt, Georg	08/10/36	20/07/37	
Nadler, Fritz	01/11/36	05/11/37	
Opitz, Ernst	08/10/36	19/07/37	
Ott, Erwin	01/06/37	09/04/38	
Panhans, Gerhard	01/10/37	25/12/37	
Paulick, Horst	01/11/36	03/10/37	
Peitz, Alfred	08/10/36	20/07/37	
Pillath, Fritz	01/09/37	31/05/39	
Poloczek, Franz	01/10/37	31/05/39	
Posselt, Martin	08/10/36	14/05/37	

Prielipp, Hans	08/10/36	20/07/37	
Reinicke, Bruno	08/10/36	03/10/37	
Reuscher, Walter	08/10/36	01/07/37	
Riedel, Heinz	08/10/36	09/08/37	01/05/37 moved to *Academia de Infantería*
Roehle, Willi	08/10/36	01/07/37	
Roever, Ewald	08/10/36	14/08/37	
Sachse, Helmuth	08/10/36	31/05/39	01/05/37 moved to *Academia de Infantería*
Sauff, Gustav	08/10/36	14/05/37	
Schaeffer, Richard	08/10/36	20/07/37	
Schaeffner, Karl	08/10/36	26/02/37	
Scharla, Kurt	08/10/36	05/11/37	01/06/37 moved to *Academia de Infantería*
Schmallandt, Otto	01/09/37	31/05/39	
Schmehl, Georg	08/10/36	31/05/39	01/06/37 moved to *Academia de Infantería*
Schmidt, Hugo	08/10/36	27/11/36	
Schmidt, Gerhard	08/10/36	21/10/37	01/06/37 became anti-tank Instructor
Schmidtinger, Jakob	08/10/36	15/11/37	01/06/37 moved to *Academia de Infantería*
Schmiegil, Johannes	08/10/36	05/03/37	
von Schmude, Otto	01/10/37	31/05/39	
Schneider, Gottfried	08/10/36	14/08/37	
Schneider, Wilhelm	08/10/36	25/07/37	
Schneider, Paul-Wilhelm	08/10/36	05/01/37	Killed in accident 05/01/37
Schoenborn, Horst	08/10/36	05/11/37	
Schrei, Otto	08/10/36	16/12/37	01/06/37 moved to *Academia de Infantería*
Schreiber, Heinz	01/06/37	31/05/39	01/08/37 moved to *Academia de Infantería*
Schroeder, Horst	08/10/36	01/07/37	
Schubert, Wilhelm	01/10/37	02/05/38	
Schulz, Erich	08/10/36	20/07/37	
Schweetzky, Emil	01/09/37	02/05/38	
Sorge, Karl Heinz	08/10/36	01/07/37	
Sparberg, Günther	08/10/36	05/11/37	
Staedtke,	08/10/36	12/12/36	
Staehr, Ewald	08/10/36	01/12/37	01/06/37 moved to *Academia de Infantería*
Stanneck, Adolf	01/11/36	01/07/37	
Stein, Kurt	08/10/36	01/12/37	01/06/37 moved to *Academia de Infantería*
Strengbier, Wilhelm	08/10/36	26/02/37	
Teige, Heinz	08/10/36	15/11/37	
Thom, Willi	08/10/36	03/10/37	
Tiefner, Alfred	08/10/36	20/07/37	
Unger, Rudolf	08/10/36	20/07/37	
Vocke, Otto	08/10/36	20/07/37	
Voelker, Erwin	08/10/36	14/08/37	01/06/37 moved to *Academia de Infantería*
Vogel, Erwin	01/10/37	25/12/37	
Vogt, Rudolf	08/10/36	09/08/37	
Voigt, Kurt	08/10/36	15/11/37	
Wagner, Edi	01/11/36	05/11/37	
Wegener, Wilhelm	08/10/36	09/02/38	01/05/37 moved to *Academia de Infantería*
Wehmann, Robert	01/09/37	02/05/38	Instructor on captured Russian tanks
Wilkniss, Hermann	08/10/36	03/10/37	
Witt, Otto	08/10/36	01/07/37	
Wohlgemuth, Fritz	08/10/36	31/08/37	KIA (Monedero)
Wuensch, Erich	08/10/36	15/11/37	Instructor on captured Russian tanks
Zipplies, Erich	08/10/36	02/12/37	01/05/37 moved to *Academia de Infantería*

TANK INSTRUCTOR SGTs

NAME	JOINED	LEFT	REMARKS
Altendorf, Wilhelm	08/10/36	01/07/37	
Auerbach, Paul	08/10/36	01/07/37	
Breit, Friedrich	01/11/36	01/07/37	
Brendel, Hans	01/11/36	01/07/37	
Bruns, Franz	08/10/36	28/02/37	
Deinzer, Hans	01/11/36	01/07/37	
Denninger, Hans	08/10/36	01/07/37	
Dettloff, Otto	08/10/36	01/07/37	
Hassfurther, Ludwig	01/06/37	12/12/37	
Heeg, Josef	01/11/36	05/11/37	
Heinz, Michael	01/11/36	01/07/38	
Heiss, Willi	08/10/36	25/05/37	
Hefer, Karl	01/11/36	01/07/37	
Hof, Karl	01/11/36	23/05/37	KIA (Durango) *Panzer I*
Kessler, Josef	01/09/37	09/04/38	
Kischnik, Arno	08/10/36	01/07/37	
Kretschmar, Walter	01/11/36	01/07/37	
Krothe, Herbert	08/10/36	01/07/37	
Kuerbis, Heinz	01/11/36	01/07/37	
Michel, Jakob	01/11/36	01/07/37	
Munchow, Horst	08/10/36	01/07/37	
Nehrhoff, Wolfgang	08/10/36	01/07/37	
Oertel, Gerhard	01/11/36	17/08/37	01/05/37 moved to *Academia de Infantería*
Schaeter, Karl	01/11/36	22/01/37	KIA 22/01/37
Scharf, Julius	08/10/36	26/04/37	
Schmidt, Hugo	08/10/36	14/05/37	
Szymanski, Heinrich	08/10/36	14/12/36	Killed in accident 14/12/37
Weber, Hugo	01/11/36	20/08/37	01/05/37 moved to *Academia de Infantería*
Worch, Franz	08/10/36	01/07/37	

SANITARY ORDERLIES ASSIGNED TO TANKS UNITS

NAME	JOINED	LEFT	REMARKS
Bernardt, Alfreed	01/10/37	02/05/38	
Gleser, Werner	08/10/36	01/12/37	
Graf, Werner	08/10/36	03/10/37	
Helmchen, Georg	01/10/37	31/05/39	
Hilke, Werner	08/10/36	07/11/37	
Maass, Siegfried	01/10/37	31/05/39	

(J.M. Campesino via Raúl Arias)

GRUPPE DROHNE STAFF PERSONNEL

NAME	JOINED	LEFT	RANK	REMARKS
Baetz, Gustav	01/09/37	31/05/39	W/O	
Bartz, Ernst	08/10/36	31/05/39	W/O	
Bischoff, Walter	01/06/37	31/05/39	W/O	
Blaich, Albert	01/10/37	31/05/39	W/O	
Bleiber, Helmuth	01/10/37	09/04/38	W/O	
Blum, Jakob	08/10/36	01/07/37	Sgt	
Brennecke, Martin	01/04/38	31/05/39	W/O	
Casper, Willi	08/10/36	03/10/37	W/O	
Dettbarn, Huwald	08/10/36	15/11/37	W/O	
Duerhagen, Werner	01/04/38	31/05/39	Sgt	
Dummer, H.Joachim	08/10/36	01/07/37	Sgt	
Ebert, Helmut	08/10/36	01/07/37	Sgt	
Eisele, Johann	01/04/38	31/05/39	W/O	
Epmeier, Fritz	01/10/37	31/05/39	Sgt	
Ferschen, Walter	01/04/38	31/05/39	Sgt	
Fertsch, Emil	01/06/37	09/04/38	W/O	
Flemming, Rudolf	08/10/36	21/10/37	2/Lt	
Von Gersdorff, Rupert	01/10/37	09/04/38	W/O	
Giese, Walter	01/11/37	31/05/39	Sgt	
Goerlitz, Fritz	01/06/37	09/04/38	W/O	
Goevel, Otto	01/10/37	15/02/38	W/O	
Gottschalk, Alfred	01/02/37	31/05/39	Interpreter	
Guenther, Paul	08/10/36	31/05/39	W/O	
Haensel, Otto	08/10/36	01/07/37	W/O	
Hampel, Paul	01/04/38	31/05/39	Sgt	
Hartdegen, Alexander	01/01/37	01/07/37	Sgt	
Herbst, Rudolf	01/04/38	31/05/39	2/Lt	
Herrmann, Johann	08/10/36	09/08/37	W/O	01/05/37 moved to *Academia de Infanteria*
Herzfeldt, Hans	01/10/37	31/05/39	W/O	
Hessenbruch, Rudolf	01/10/37	31/05/39	Sgt	
Holzner, Eduard	01/10/37	31/05/39	W/O	
Huewe, Heinrich	08/10/36	01/07/37	Sgt	
Jakob, Helmuth	08/10/36	15/11/37	W/O	
Kaempfe, Dietrich	08/10/36	01/07/37	Sgt	
Kerstan, Alfred	08/10/36	15/11/37	W/O	
Von Kirchbach, Adalbert	08/10/36	15/11/37	W/O	
Koch, Erich	01/09/37	31/05/39	W/O	
Kowaczek, Erich	01/10/37	31/05/39	W/O	
Kroos, Anton	01/10/37	09/04/38	W/O	
Krueger, Hans-Joachim	08/10/36	01/07/37	Sgt	
Kuehl, Detlef	01/04/38	31/05/39	W/O	
Lechner, Nikolaus	01/02/38	31/05/39	Sgt	
Leischke, Walter	08/10/36	21/10/37	W/O	
Liewald, Kurt	01/04/38	31/05/39	W/O	
Maurer, Otto	08/10/36	01/07/37	Sgt	
Meiners, Kurt	01/04/38	31/05/39	W/O	
Nowitzki, Fritz	01/04/38	31/05/39	Sgt	
Von Ostmann, Eberhard	08/10/36	29/08/37	Lt Col	01/05/37 moved to *Academia de Infanteria*
Pechan, Walter	01/10/37	31/05/39	W/O	
Pelzer, Hans	23/09/36	31/12/37	Interpreter	
Pinkwart, Hans	08/10/36	15/11/37	W/O	

Rabe, Kurt	01/09/37	09/04/38	W/O	
Reibig, Willi	08/10/36	01/07/37	2/Lt	
Richter, Gerhard	08/10/36	01/12/37	W/O	01/05/37 moved to *Academia de Infantería*
Rudolph, Herbert	08/10/36	02/05/38	W/O	
Ruemmler, Johannes	08/10/36	15/11/37	Sgt	
Scbirey, Heinz	01/04/38	31/05/39	Sgt	
Scheuern, Georg	08/10/36	03/11/37	W/O	KIA 03/11/37 (Burgos)
Schneider, Paul	01/04/38	02/05/38	W/O	
Schreiber, Fritz	01/09/37	31/05/37	Sgt	
Schreiter, Heinz	08/10/36	15/11/37	W/O	
Schulze, Herbert	08/10/36	15/11/37	W/O	
Soehnitz, Walter	01/09/37	02/05/38	W/O	
Soffge, Gerhard	08/10/36	01/07/37	Sgt	
Sternkopf, Werner	01/04/38	31/05/38	Sgt	
Stoelzel, Hans	01/10/37	02/05/38	W/O	
Suessespeck, Kurt	01/11/37	31/05/39	2/Lt	
Thissen, Hubert	01/09/37	31/05/39	Sgt	
Thomas, Siegfried	08/10/36	15/11/37	W/O	
Thomas, Eberhard	01/09/37	31/05/39	W/O	
Utpatel, Karl Heinz	01/09/37	31/05/39	W/O	
Wald, Karl	01/04/38	31/05/39	W/O	
Welzel, Rudolf	08/10/36	30/11/36	W/O	
Wichler, Reinhold	08/10/36	21/10/37	2/Lt	
Wistuba, Alfred	01/04/38	31/05/39	W/O	
Wolkes, Waldemar	01/04/38	31/05/39	Sgt	
Zemelka, Heinz	08/10/36	15/11/37	2/Lt	
Zimny, Franz	01/04/38	31/05/39	Sgt	

GRUPPE DROHNE MEDICAL COs AND OFFICERS

NAME	JOINED	LEFT	RANK	REMARKS
Engelhardt, Johannes	08/10/36	01/08/37	Maj	
Esselbruegge, Hermann	01/03/38	01/05/39	Maj	
Roessner, Hans	01/07/37	09/04/38	Capt	

GRUPPE DROHNE QUARTERMASTER COs AND OFFICERS

NAME	JOINED	LEFT	RANK	REMARKS
Franzbach, Max	01/05/37	31/05/39	Capt	
Muehlenkamp, Fritz	08/10/36	15/05/37	Maj	

LEGIÓN CÓNDOR INTERPRETERS ASSIGNED TO *GRUPPE DROHNE*

NAME	JOINED	LEFT	RANK	REMARKS
Nagel, Werner	01/09/37	31/05/39	2/Lt	
Proessdorf, Walter	01/04/38	31/05/39	W/O	
Schwemke, Walter	08/10/36	09/08/37	W/O	

GRUPPE DROHNE ANTI-TANK UNIT PERSONNEL

NAME	JOINED	LEFT	RANK	REMARKS
Ehlert, Werner	01/09/37	31/05/39	Sgt	
Fitzak, Hans	01/06/37	31/05/39	NCO	
Haupt, Kurt	01/06/37	31/05/39	W/O	
Jansa, Peter	01/11/36	18/03/38	Maj	Unit CO
Kohse, Arnold	01/06/37	31/05/39	W/O	
Nethe, Gerhard	08/10/36	15/11/37	2/Lt	
Novak, Hans	08/10/36	03/10/37	W/O	
Rieschick, Karl	08/10/36	31/05/39	2/Lt	
Seifert, Johann	08/10/36	09/08/37	W/O	
Ullrich, Hugo	08/10/36	15/11/37	W/O	
Vermeulen, Johann	08/10/36	31/05/39	2/Lt	
Wieseler, Josef	08/10/36	31/05/39	Interpreter	
Winterer, Otto	01/09/37	26/12/37	Sgt	
Wolf, Martin	01/11/36	09/08/37	W/O	

Willibald Schmidt, one of the *Gruppe Drohne* interpreters. In this case, it is the *Dolmetscher* of the *Panzer Gruppe* Workshop. (J.M. Campesino via Raúl Arias)

GRUPPE DROHNE TRANSPORT COMPANY PERSONNEL

NAME	JOINED	LEFT	RANK	REMARKS
Adametz, Paul	08/10/36	01/07/37	Sgt	
Alexejew, Eugen	08/10/36	01/07/37	Sgt	
Brass, Heinrich	08/10/36	16/12/37	W/O	
Buchta, Willi	01/06/37	14/09/37	Sgt	
Cherwinski, Fritz	08/10/36	16/12/37	W/O	
Damm, Albert	01/06/37	31/05/39	W/O	
Dienemann, Erich	01/06/37	31/05/39	W/O	15/12/37 joined Staff
Dreyer, Willi	08/10/36	12/12/37	W/O	
Eisold, Herbert	08/10/36	01/07/37	Sgt	
Feuer, Heinrich	08/10/36	31/05/39	Mechanic	
Foerster, K.arl-Heinz	08/10/36	02/04/37	Sgt	Died of illness (Cubas)
Goeggelmann, Hans	01/06/37	31/05/39	W/O	
Graefe, Karl	08/10/36	04/05/37	W/O	
Guder, Willi	01/06/37	01/12/37	W/O	
Habermehl, Paul	08/10/36	17/08/37	W/O	
Haenel, Sigfried	08/10/36	01/07/37	Sgt	
Hunger, Georg	08/10/36	01/07/37	Sgt	
Janne, Gerhard	08/10/36	12/12/37	W/O	
Krause, Ernst	08/10/36	12/12/37	2/Lt	
Marquis, Erich	08/10/36	01/07/37	Sgt	
Meyer, Walter	08/10/36	31/05/39	W/O	
Milkowski, Hans	01/02/37	30/09/37	Interpreter	
Mirfanger, Emil	08/10/36	31/05/39	W/O	
Moede, Oscar	08/10/36	16/12/37	W/O	
Nagel, Karl	01/06/37	31/05/39	Sgt	
Nowak, Heinz	08/10/36	19/07/37	Sgt	
Proebius, Otto	08/10/36	12/12/37	W/O	
Przyklenk, Wilhelm	08/10/36	12/12/37	W/O	
Richter, Alfred	01/06/37	31/05/39	W/O	01/01/38 joined Staff
Ruhland, Karl	08/10/36	12/12/37	W/O	
Rusch, Walter	08/10/36	16/12/37	W/O	
Schmidt, Gustav	08/10/36	09/04/38	2/Lt	01/01/38 joined Staff
Schmitz, Josef	08/10/36	31/05/39	Mechanic	
Schroeter, Max	08/10/36	01/07/37	2/Lt	
Schruefer, Hans	08/10/36	31/05/39	Capt	Coy CO
Singer, Helmut	08/10/36	12/12/37	W/O	
Sporbert, Willi	08/10/36	07/01/37	Sgt	
Stockhausen, Johannes	01/06/37	02/05/38	W/O	01/12/37 joined Staff
Thamm, Willi	08/10/36	01/12/37	2/Lt	
Trapp, Hans	01/06/37	25/12/37	Sgt	01/12/37 joined Staff
Trentsch, Alfred	08/10/36	12/12/37	W/O	
Vietmeyer, Werner	08/10/36	07/02/37	2/Lt	
Weiss, Johann	08/10/36	24/11/37	W/O	
Wendt, Wilhelm	01/06/37	01/12/37	2/Lt	
Wenzel, Bruno	01/06/37	12/12/37	W/O	
Wladarz, Werner	08/10/36	01/07/37	W/O	
Wolter, Wilhelm	08/10/36	16/12/37	2/Lt	
Zefahrt, Josef	08/10/36	16/12/37	W/O	
Ziegenbalg, Friedrich	01/06/37	05/10/37	Sgt	

GRUPPE DROHNE WORKSHOP PERSONNEL

NAME	JOINED	LEFT	RANK	REMARKS
Angerer, Wilhelm	08/10/36	01/07/37	Mechanic	06/37 moved to *Academia de Infantería*
Berger, Rudolf	08/10/36	01/07/37	Mechanic	
Beyermann, Otto	08/10/36	01/07/37	Mechanic	
Blaszcinski, Franz	08/10/36	01/07/37	Mechanic	
Boelke, Wilhelm	08/10/36	01/07/37	Mechanic	
Delzeit, Heinrich	01/09/37	31/05/39	W/O	
Doerschmann, Alfred	08/10/36	31/05/39	W/O	01/05/37 moved to *Academia de Infantería*
Dohr, Heinz	01/09/37	31/05/39	W/O	
Ehrlich, Fritz	08/10/36	21/10/37	W/O	
Fuerst, Paul	08/10/36	09/08/37	2/Lt	
Goetz, Franz	01/11/36	31/05/39	Interpreter	
Gorges, Peter	01/04/38	31/05/39	Sgt	
Hagenauer, Erich	08/10/36	15/11/37	W/O	
Heinrich, Otto	01/10/37	31/05/39	W/O	
Jaskula, Bruno	08/10/36	01/07/37	Mechanic	Specialist
Jaskula, Paul	01/10/36	30/04/37	Lt	Workhop CO. Killed in air crash
Linke, Erich	08/10/36	01/07/37	Mechanic	Specialist
Luebke, Werner	08/10/36	01/07/37	Mechanic	Specialist
Mueller, Hugo	08/10/36	15/11/37	W/O	
Schmidt, Willibald	08/10/36	01/12/37	Interpreter	
Schneider, Albert	01/11/36	31/05/39	Capt	
Schnell, Fedor	08/10/36	30/04/37	W/O	
Schwarzer, Kurt	08/10/36	03/10/37	W/O	
Singer, Martin	08/10/36	31/05/39	W/O	
Sprung, Heinz	01/10/37	31/05/38	W/O	
Striehn, Willi	08/10/36	15/11/37	W/O	01/07/37 joined Staff
Weimann, Ernst	08/10/36	01/07/37	Mechanic	
Winkel, Ferdinand	08/10/36	01/07/37	Mechanic	

GRUPPE DROHNE ARMOURY PERSONNEL

NAME	JOINED	LEFT	RANK	REMARKS
Albert, Ludwig	01/10/37	31/05/39	Armourer	
Bruch, Heinz	01/09/37	31/05/39	Sgt	
Gajdzinski, Fritz	01/10/37	25/12/37	Sgt	
Gerson, Oskar	08/10/36	15/11/37	W/O	
Hanfler, Richard	08/10/36	16/12/37	Armourer	
Hoffmann, Gottfried	01/10/37	31/05/39	2/Lt	
Kleiner, Georg	01/06/37	31/05/39	2/Lt	
Klopsch, Otto	08/10/36	09/08/37	2/Lt	
Koch, Erich	08/10/36	07/11/37	2/Lt	
Kummer, Horst	08/10/36	09/04/38	W/O	
Nagel, Werner	01/09/37	31/05/39	2/Lt	
Proessdorf, Walter	01/04/38	31/05/39	W/O	
Schwemke, Walter	08/10/36	09/08/37	W/O	

GRUPPE DROHNE MEMBERS AT INFANTRY ACADEMIES

NAME	JOINED	LEFT	RANK	REMARKS
Dietz, Edwin	01/11/37	31/05/39	W/O	*Academia de Infantería*
Hoffmann, Walter	01/10/37	31/05/39	W/O	*Academia de Infantería*

Erwin Voelker and Paul Erman of *Panzer Gruppe Thoma*. (J.M. Campesino via Raúl Arias)

7

Miscellaneous

Gruppe Drohne Uniforms

When they arrived in Spain, the German soldiers were wearing civilian clothes, the same they had been wearing on their "leisure" trip from their country to Seville on the SS *Girgenti* and SS *Pasajes*. On the first days, they were issued fatigue uniforms and black berets.

And thus they started the training of the Spanish recruits, whose uniforms, in many cases, were not any better. In any case, during their stay at the base at Las Herguijuelas, the search for more suitable clothing for their military functions started.

In October 1936 they were given the new uniform, which consisted of a khaki tunic and trousers, pale khaki shirt, woollen 3/4 overcoat with two rows of buttons (khaki as well), and a black beret. The belt and the straps were pale leather, like the shirt, for warrant officers, and black or hazelnut leather for chief officers and officers. Finally, the pistol holster—that all of them were carryin—was black leather.

These were the uniforms in the first months. However, like the Spaniards, they used to wear green-grey or blue fatigue uniforms when they were in the tanks, although in this case, the color array could be really spectacular depending on various factors, like the number of washings, or the model acquired.

In the early days after their arrival in Spanish territory, *Panzer Gruppe Drohne* men used to wear overalls and a black beret. (J.M. Campesino via Raúl Arias)

Shortly afterwards, in December, the last and definitive *Gruppe Thoma* service and dress uniform was distributed, similar to the one used by the air contingent of the *Legión Cóndor*, although with particular shades. The tunic was khaki, open, and with four pockets: two on the chest and another two on the lower part. On the upper left pocket were the rank badges (stars for officers and gallons for warrant oficers). Pinned on the left pocket—those who had the right to use it—and worn with pride was the *Gruppe Drohne* special badge, a skull and a tank surrounded with oak leaves. Some tunics had epaulettes (quite often officers' tunics did so), although most lacked them.

The trousers, besides, were khaki and could be straight, along with black shoes, or "breeches," used with top or riding boots, and even with leggings. The shirt was pale chickpea and had upper pockets; weather permitting, the rank badges were worn on it. The tie was black.

The most important distinctive element the *Gruppe Drohne* men used to wear were black berets, on which the Germans put the skull, the *Panzer* troops badge, and, in most cases, under the latter, the swastika, the emblem of German National Socialism. At the beginning, some Germans used rank badges on their berets, like the Spanish tank crews, who always wore the stars or gallons under the skull—which they also used to wear.

In this night snapshot, the members of the *2ª Compañía* of the *Panzer Gruppe Drohne*, wearing a transition uniform, listen to the radio, the only link with the fatherland. (J.M. Campesino via Raúl Arias)

Top: left to right, *alféreces* Tegel and Ainoza, *Oberleutnant* Bothe, *capitán* Losada, interpreter Drechsel, and *Oberleutnant* Willing posing at Orduña after a reconnaissance of the terrain to prepare a surprise attack (May 1937). Bottom: *capitán* Gonzalo Díez de la Lastra, CO of the *3ª Compañía de Carros*, posing with two Germans and an interpreter (*Dolmetscher*) of the *Legión Cóndor*. (both J.M. Campesino via Raúl Arias)

Top: *Unteroffizier* Hans Joachim Freitag.
Next page, top: *comandante* Pujales and some of his men talking to some *Drohne* men.
Next page, bottom: several *Panzer Gruppe* men chatting at a mobile canteen of their aviation comrades.
(J.M. Campesino via Raúl Arias)

The *Panzertruppenabzeichen der Legion Condor*

By mid November 1936, *Oberstleutnant* Wilhelm von Thoma established a special badge that characterized all the members of the tank contingent of the *Legión Cóndor—Panzer Gruppe Drohne*—out of other instructors of the German unit in Spain. The men who were entitled to wear this insignia on their uniforms were the *Drohne* Germans who had stayed in Spain as instructors for at least three months, showing good conduct during that period. Bearing in mind that there were 423 men serving in the *Panzer Gruppe Drohne* during the entire war, it seems that the figure of 415 men so distinguished, as reported by Dr Klietmann back in 1957 in an article published in the bimonthly magazine "The Medal Collector," was quite close to the facts.

The insignia consisted of a skull with two tibias behind—the symbol of the German armored troops, from the old Hussars and Chasseurs regiments—on a generic representation of a tank, surrounded with oak leaves.

Although the first ones were cast in silver, they were so vulnerable to wear-and-tear that it forced a change for the rest to a tougher silvery pressed metal.

The insignia was pinned on the left pocket of the tunic by means of a vertical clip.

(via Manuel Álvaro)

Right to left: *General der Flieger* Hugo Sperrle, *Oberstleutnant* Wilhelm von Thoma, *Oberleutnant* Hermann Aldinger, and *Hauptmann* Lieb talking on the Bilbao Front. June 1937. (J.M. Campesino via Raúl Arias)

(via Manuel Álvaro)

Oberstleutnant Hans Freiherr von Funck, head of *Gruppe Imker* and German Military Attaché in Nationalist Spain, and Wilhelm Ritter von Thoma, head of *Gruppe Drohne* and of the German instructors in Spain, watching the artillery fire on the San Roque bunker (the last position before Bilbao), June 1937. Notice the most curious way of holding the binoculars—with a branch suitably peeled and without leaves—of the head of the tank contingent. (J.M. Campesino via Raúl Arias)

Top: *Oberstleutnant* von Funck with his interpreter, Vollrath, at Herguijuelas Castle, Cáceres. (J.M. Campesino via Raúl Arias) Bottom: machine gun fire practice with the *Panzer I* at Cubas. (Authors)

For driving training, the Germans sent a *Panzerkampfwagen I Ausf. A "ohne aufbau,"* i.e. "without superstructure," to Spain. As it can be seen in the views, apart from the instructor and the trainee driver, several other trainees could be sitting on the sides of the vehicle. (Authors)

Gruppe Drohne casualties

Although the German tank crew contingent—like the rest of their comrades of the *Heer*—was not a fighting unit, several of its members died or were killed in action, which gives an idea how committed, intense, and dangerous the collaboration of *Gruppe Drohne* was. Besides those killed in action, there were also accidents that members of the tank unit of the German Army were involved in. Others, unfortunately, died of illness.

W/O Arnold Kasulke, of *Panzer Gruppe Drohne*, having breakfast at the base at Las Herguijuelas, Cáceres. (J.M. Campesino via Raúl Arias)

Different tank training scenes of *Panzer Gruppe Drohne*. All the types of German tanks in service in the Nationalist Army can be seen in these practice exercises: *Panzerkampfwagen I*, *Panzerbefehlswagen I*, and *Panzer I "ohne aufbau" I*. (top: J.M. Campesino via Raúl Arias; bottom: Authors)

Here follows a review of those who lost their lives in Spain.

During the ofensive on Bilbao, in May 1937, the *Drohne* lost its first men in action. These were the tank instructor W/O Adalbert Butz of the 3 Company, killed on 12 May at Murga, Biscay, shot in the head, and tank instructor Sgt Karl Hof, killed on the 23rd of that same month on the Durango front, Biscay, when the tank he was driving was hit by an anti-tank gun shell.

Only two months later, on 24 July, this time in the Battle of Brunete, *Panzer Gruppe Drohne* recorded its third combat casualty. This was a Section CO 1st lieutenant of the 2 *Panzerkompanie*, Hans Hannibal von Moerner, who was killed on a reconnaissance sortie of his section near the village of Brunete, Madrid.

On 16 April 1938, it was the chief of the *Legión Cóndor* himself—by this time, it was *General* Volkmann—who sent the Generalissimo's HQs an official letter asking for the awarding of a posthumous *Medalla Militar Individual* to 1/Lt von Moerner, for "...he drove his tank in combat in a most exemplary way for his Spanish and German comrades of the armored troops. For his daring reconnaissance sorties, particularly in war operations, he became very popular among the moorish and legionnaire troops, particularly on the Madrid front."

On the 21st of the same month, the *Negociado de Recompensas* of the *3ª Sección del Estado Mayor del C.G.G* (Awards Department), bearing in mind the records mentioned in the letter by the chief of the *Legión Cóndor*, proposed the awarding of the decoration, which was delivered to the parents of the dead 1st lieutenant with the diploma attached.

On 24 April, and on Franco's orders, the chief general of the General Staff signed the order for the awarding, which said:

> "Bearing in mind the merits and circumstances, which are listed overleaf, pertaining to '*negrillo*' 1/Lt HANS HANNIBAL VON MOERNER, killed for our Cause at Brunete on 26 (sic) July 1937, I have decided to award him the *Medalla Militar*, Which I notify to Y.E. for your knowledge and purposes. This award must not be published.
>
> Let God protect Y.E. for many years
> Burgos, 24 April 1938
> II Triumphant Year"

Leutnant Hans Hannibal von Moerner, KIA at Brunete and decorated with the *Medalla Militar*. (J.M. Campesino via Raúl Arias)

A memorial stone to honor W/O Georg Scheuern of the *Gruppe Thoma* staff, wounded on a front patrol at Cangas de Onís, Asturias, on 12 October 1937, and died on 3 November at the *Hospital Militar* in Burgos.

On 31 August 1937, tank instructor W/O Fritz Wohlgemuth died on the Santander front. He was hit several times while on an operation carried out at the Muñorrodero tunnel, Santander.

The end of 1937 was nearing when, on 3 November, *Drohne* Staff W/O Georg Scheuern died at the Military Hospital in Burgos. The month before he had been hit by enemy fire in the stomach at the Cangas de Onís municipality, Asturias, while on a reconnaissance patrol.

The last casualty was Captain Gustav Trippe, deputy chief of the only tank training company of *Gruppe Drohne* still in Spain in November 1938. The Battle of the Ebro was coming to an end at La Fatarella sierra, when this captain died on a reconnaissance sortie carried out by the tank unit he was accompanying.

Gruppe Thoma had five accident casualties and two died of illness, which makes a total of thirteen losses in the group during the Spanish conflict. Three of the accident casualties were in vehicle or motorcycle crashes, a fourth one was killed by a stray rifle bullet from a comrade, and the fifth one, Paul Jaskula, was killed in an unfortunate air crash on 30 April 1937. On that day, the courier plane on the Seville-Rome route got lost, probably in the Malaga area. The wreck was never found. Jaskula was a *Werkmeister* (workshop chief), and was regarded as a highly reputed specialist in armored equipment repairs.

The two illness casualties, a tank instructor W/O and a member of the transport company, both were victims of heart strokes during 1937.

PANZER GRUPPE DROHNE PERSONNEL KIA

NAME	RANK	DATE	PLACE	POSTING	REMARKS
Butz, Adalbert	NCO	12/05/37	Murga	Instructor	Shot in the head
Hof, Karl	Sgt	23/05/37	Durango	Instructor	Killed in tank combat
Von Moerner, H. Hannibal	Lt	24/07/37	Brunete	Section CO	Killed in tank combat
Wohlgemuth, Fritz	NCO	31/08/37	Muñorrodero	Instructor	Defending a tunnel
Scheuern, Georg	NCO	03/11/37	Burgos	Staff	Shot in the stomach, Asturias
Trippe, Gustav	Capt	14/11/38	Fatarella	Coy CO	Armed reconnaissance

PANZER GRUPPE DROHNE PERSONNEL KILLED IN ACCIDENT

NAME	RANK	DATE	PLACE	POSTING	REMARKS
Kempe, Paul	NCO	09/10/36	Cáceres	Instructor	Car crash
Szymansky, Heinrich	Sgt	14/12/36	Madrid	Instructor	Car crash
Schaefer, Karl	Sgt	22/01/37	Cubas	Instructor	Rifle accidentally shot by mate
Schneider, Paul Wilhelm	NCO	31/08/37	Germany	Instructor	Motorcycle crash
Jaskula, Paul	Lt	30/04/37	Burgos	Workshop Chief	Seville-Rome air courier crash

PANZER GRUPPE DROHNE PERSONNEL DIED OF ILLNESS

NAME	RANK	DATE	PLACE	POSTING	REMARKS
Foerster, Karl Heinz	Sgt	02/04/37	Cubas	Transport Coy	Heart stroke
Balewsky, Otto	NCO	24/07/37	Cubas	Instructor	Heart stroke

The other Germans

Besides all these Germans of the *Heer* who were part of *Panzer Gruppe Drohne* on Spanish soil during the 1936 civil conflict, there were also others. Although this is a much less important matter than the history of *Gruppe Drohne* itself and certainly very little publicized so far, there were some Germans who were serving in *La Legión*, or were living in Spain who applied for a posting, or asked to collaborate with von Thoma's tank crew group. What is more, there were some Germans still in their own country who asked the Nationalist authorities permission to take part in the conflict with their Army comrades.

A tank carrier truck of the *Panzer Gruppe Drohne* Transport Company, crossing a bridge while several Germans of the *Gruppe* watch from the river, relaxing and having a bath. (J.M. Campesino via Raúl Arias)

There were not many, certainly, but if we failed to mention them here, the history would be incomplete. Their case, in our opinion, is a very curious and illustrative one.

As it is well known, *La Legión*, or *El Tercio*, as it was known in its early days, admitted foreigners in its ranks, with no limitations. And from the start many foreigners of all classes and social condition decided to volunteer and join the best Spanish assault troops of all time.

By late September 1936, several Germans who had joined *El Tercio* before the war were selected to be posted to the German tank unit, the recently established *Gruppe Drohne*. Despite likely omissions, there were the following *caballeros legionarios* (legionnaire gentlemen): *alférez* Otto Preil, *sargento* Virgilio Arens and soldiers Alois Loira, Ferdinand Kaiser, F. Hartzkhon, Juan D. Kozki, Luis Retract, and Victor Kissenberger. By mid-November, several German-speaking legionnaires, including Hermann Reichlmeier, Karl Haas, Burkhardt Stein, Kurt Geisel, Josef Riesinger, and Johann Eckschmidt also joined.

Of those who joined in November, the first four belonged to the *28ª Compañía* of the *7ª Bandera*, the fifth one was part of the *32ª Compañía* of the *8ª Bandera*, and the last one belonged to the *Compañía Lanzallamas* (Flamethrower Company) of the *2ª Legión*. All of them, except Eckschmidt, were posted at Cubas, attached to the *Sección de instrucción de carros de combate* (Tank Training Section). Their command of the Spanish language was probably very useful to von Thoma.

In any case, these six German legionnaires, along with another four of the same nationality, were prematurely discharged in July 1937 after German Ambassador Faupel had earnestly asked the Generalissimo's HQs.

Legionnaires Erich Raupach, A. Rechnitzer, F. Sieger, Hans Frei, Eugen Berger, and Johan Lonch also served in tanks and anti-tank guns.

An Sd.Ah 115 tank carrier platform. The Transport Company of *Panzer Gruppe Drohne* used nineteen during the war. (Authors)

Cubas de la Sagra, a village very close to Madrid, was the place chosen by the *Panzer Gruppe* to establish the Staff services, and tank school during the Spanish Civil War. (J.M. Campesino via Raúl Arias)

Above: A *Panzer Gruppe Drohne* Workshop at Cuatro Vientos. In the picture, a Renault FT-17 captured from the Republicans and, in the background, two Avro 504 aircraft found by the Nationalists in the hangars when the latter were captured. (J.M. Campesino via Raúl Arias) Left: Spare barrels for the German 37-mm Pak 35/36 anti-tank guns. (Authors)

A curious case is that of a legionnaire of German origin, Enrique Schommer, who joined *La Legión* in March 1937 and was posted to the Spanish tank unit. In September, von Thoma asked the *Jefatura de M.I.R.* for this legionnaire to be admitted to the course for temporary second lieutenants announced for the Fuencaliente Academy, Burgos, along with a Russian citizen called Igor von Sakharow, who had also volunteered for *El Tercio*. Orgaz agreed to the request, and on 24 November both passed the course and were promoted to the corresponding rank "for the duration." Schommer and his comrade were posted to the *Batallón de Carros de combate* of the *Regimiento de Carros nº 2*, a unit where they served the entire war, under its different designations.

A few months later, a German citizen of whom we only know his family name, Winterer, applied to volunteer in the conflict, attached to the Nationalist anti-tank units. But unlike many other foreigners who applied to volunteer in Franco's Army, in this case, his application was backed by a report from *Oberstleutnant* von Funck that said as follows:

> "This it to certify that the German citizen WINTERER can serve as a volunteer in a Spanish anti-tank gun company.
>
> He is to be paid by the *Legión Cóndor* and no responsibilities or compromise are incurred by the Spanish State."

We guess *Herr* Winterer must have joined the Spanish anti-tank units.

It was the opposite with the German J. Krug, a warrant officer of the disbursing office and administration of the German Army during the First World War, who volunteered on 1 March 1939 for the administration of the German volunteer troops of the *Heer*, who was not admitted despite his records. The nearing end of the war, as well as the lack of a favorable report from the German liaison officer at the C.G.G. ruined the hopes of this German citizen to fight against communism in the Nationalist Army.

The German national J. Krug asked to be accepted in Franco's Army as a specialist in military administration matters. (Authors)

The case of a German who had become naturalized as Spanish, Andrés Otto Volck is even more interesting. A resident in Spain and a metal engineer by profession, at the start of the Nationalist uprising he was living in Corunna, where he joined the local militia called "*Caballeros de La Coruña*,"[14] in which he served until 14 September 1936, when he volunteered to *La Legión* "for the duration."

He was injured on 13 November 1936 at the Usera neighborhood in Madrid and was in hospital until 1 February 1937. Then he joined the *Agrupación de Carros Blindados* of the *Ejército del Sur* (South Army Tank Group), in which he stayed until the establishment of the *Agrupación de carros de combate* of the same Army, which took place on 1 August 1937. Bearing in mind his merits and professional qualifications, and for service requirements, he became a temporary sergeant and took charge of the armory. In December that same year, again for service requirements, he was promoted to temporary warrant officer and was in charge of the organization and command of the *1ª Sección de Carros Orugas "Renault"* (1. Renault Track Tank Section). In February 1938, when the *Compañía de Carros Orugas* was

Victory parade in Seville. In the picture is the Russian tank Company enlisted into the *Agrupación de Carros Blindados del Ejército del Sur*. The German national Otto Volck, who had become Spanish naturalized, served in the unit. (National Library)

stablished, he remained at the *1ª Sección*, later to command the *2ª Compañia*, equipped ith Russian T-26 tanks numbered 22, 23, and 31.

He took part in the operations at Valenzuela and the tank operations on the front of Estremadura, and at the Villafranca de Córdoba and Pueblonuevo el Terrible sectors. In the ction carried out to take the Monte Rubio hills he was wounded, but refused the evacuation nd stayed in command of his section. Through his own action, three enemy armored ailway engines were destroyed: one at La Granjuela, the second one at El Helechal, and nother one in the area surrounding El Almorchón. Besides, he captured three Russian T-6B tanks, which were soon repaired and serviced by the *Agrupación* itself, and destroyed a Republican anti-tank gun in the operation carried out to take the Zalamea pass.

Andrés Otto Volck was born in Riga, Latvia, in 1894, and graduated as a metal engineer at the Mining Academy of Freiberg, Saxony, in June 1922. In November 1934 he received Spanish nationality, and had lived in Spain ever since.

In January 1938, Otto Volck applied for military assimilation as a 1st lieutenant through he CO of the Tank Unit of the *Ejército del Sur*, *capitán* Miguel Cabanellas Torres, as he hought his case adjusted to the Orders of the *Secretaría de Guerra* of 8 March 1937 (B.O. n° 141). In March that same year, the official letter from the Chief General of the *Ejército del Sur* arrived at the Generalissimo's HQs asking for assimilation, although unfortunately for him his application was turned down, stating that the Orders of the *Secretaría de Guerra* in question applied to the *Servicio de Automovilismo*[15] only.

Not discouraged by the refusal, and in order to reward Volck's good services, the chief commander of the *Agrupación de Carros de Combate* of the *Ejército del Sur* wrote a proposal in December 1938 asking for his assimilation as an honorary 1st lieutenant, and sent it again through military channels to the Generalissimo's HQs. The proposal was

(J.M. Campesino via Raúl Arias)

Despite its poor characteristics as a war weapon, the *Panzer I* was certainly a good element for the training of the Spanish soldiers in modern armored warfare. Its presence in Spain spanned over twenty years, something its designers could have never dreamt of. (Guillermo Shöbel, via Cesar O'Donnell)

turned down again by the HQs for, in accordance with the Orders of 20 July 1938, on which the request was based, the latter referred only to the granting of honorary ranks for the Artillery, Engineer, and Aviation arms, which was not the case, as he was an Infantryman.

Otto Volck's misfortune was obvious, and never went beyond temporary warrant officer rank, with enough merits for something else, but with little luck.

8

The Post-War

Once the Spanish conflict was over, and after taking part in the Victory Parade along the Paseo de la Castellana in Madrid on 19 May and the official farewell to the *Legión Cóndor*, presided over by Generalissimo Franco on 22 May 1939 at the air base of La Virgen del Camino in León, the last members of the *Drohne* still in Spain left for Vigo to board one of the ships chartered by the *Wehrmacht* to sail back to Germany with the rest of their comrades of *Gruppe Imker* and the *Legión Cóndor* itself.

Two days later, on 24 May, five huge German liners of the *Kraft durch Freude* organization—"Strength Through Joy" in English—arrived loaded with medicines, surgical equipment, and food as a present from the German *Arbeitsfront* to the Spanish state.

These ships (the *Wilhelm Gustloft*, *Robert Ley*, *Stuttgart*, *Der Deutsche*, and *Sierra*

General der Flieger von Richthofen, head of the Legión Cóndor, awarding Oberst von Thoma the Medalla Militar Individual for his participation in the 1936-39 conflict commanding the tank contingent and as a Heer instructor in Spain. (J.M. Campesino via Raúl Arias)

116

ordoba) took on board all the Germans still on Spanish soil at that time and left on the ?6ᵗʰ, destination Hamburg.

The one hundred and eight members of *Panzer Gruppe Drohne* still in Spain, along vith the instructors at the different academies, *Gruppe Wolm* (radio monitoring Company) nembers, and the *Gruppe Imker* Staff boarded the 900-passenger liner *Sierra Cordoba*, ilthough this time they numbered only 399.

The welcome in Hamburg was tremendous: *Reichsmarshall* Hermann Göring, with Keitel and Raeder—as *Heer* and *Kriegsmarine* Chief Commanders respectively—hailed :hem on behalf of the Führer. Once they landed, the troops marched past the leaders and the people of Hamburg. From there, the legionnaires were driven to the camp at Doberitz, near Berlin, to prepare the great parade of the whole unit, which was to be held before chancelor Hitler the following week.

Before the Berlin parade, on 3 June General von Brauchitsch visited the *Heer* contingent at Doberitz—the tank crews, instructors, and members of the *Horch-Truppen*—whom he harangued, and thanked them for the services provided to the German Army "in its fight against bolshevism in Spain." Then he decorated several members with the "*Cruz de España*" (Spanish Cross) in gold and silver, and promoted 51-year-old W/O (*Feldwebel*) Karl Kuebler to lieutenant. This man, who was living in Spain as the war broke out, had volunteered to fight in Franco's Army, and was transferred to *Gruppe Thoma* on 23 September 1936 to serve as an interpreter assigned to the *Panzer Gruppe* during the whole war. His courage, proved in duty, prompted the German high command to honor him in that

A *Panzerbefehlswagen* marching past a winning General Franco, Madrid, Victory Parade on 1 May 1939 (J. Mazarrasa)

Top: May 1939. The German tank crews prepare for the parade. In the foreground, Soviet T-26B tanks captured by the Nationalists and enlisted into the Nationalist armored units. (Authors) Bottom: in the port of Vigo, ready to embark, 25 May 1939. (via Francisco Marín)

(Bundesarchiv)

way, and their Spanish counterpart gave him the *Medalla de la Campaña de España 1936-1939* (Medal for the Spanish Campaign 1936-1939), the *Cruz Roja al Mérito Militar* (Red Division to the Military Order of Merit), the *Cruz de Guerra* (War Cross), and the *Medalla Militar Individual* (Military Individual Medal).

This ceremony was used to establish a commemoration in the form of a traditional cufftitle to honor the Germans of the *Heer* who fought in Spain between 1936 and 1939. It was awarded to the members of the *Panzerlehr-Regiment, Nachrichten-Lehr-Abteilung*, and *Versuchs-Abteilung* units that supplied personnel to the *Gruppe Imker* in its different training and radio monitoring tasks during the three war years. This red 32-mm wide band with the inscription "*1936 Spanien 1939*" in gothic golden letters was sewn on the right cuff of the tunic.

On 6 June, at 1000 hrs, the grand triumphant parade of the *Legión Cóndor* started in Berlin with over 18,000 men, including the crews of the battleships *Deutschland* and *Graf Spee*. They formed and marched past the greatest leaders of the German Reich, as well as a large Spanish military commission headed by *generales* Queipo de Llano, Solchaga, Aranda, and Yagüe.

After the troops' review the parade started, and all the legionnaires went through the arches of the Brandenburg Gate and walked in correct formation to the Lustgarten esplanade, where the main homage took place. There, on a platform erected for the event, Hitler and Göring addressed the public and emphasized the courage of the German volunteers in the Spanish conflict. The *Legión Cóndor* was now history.

9

The Heritage of the *Drohne* Tank Crews

According to a most interesting document of the *II Negociado* (department) of the *1ᵃ Sección de la Jefatura de M.I.R.*, dated 12 May 1939, besides the thirty-four Renault FT-17s and seventy "Gun Tanks" (captured Soviet T-26 Bs) there were eighty-four "*negrillo*" (German, *Panzerkampfwagen I*) tanks operational by that date. In the last figure—which is the most relevant for this work—a most important statistic deduction can be drawn: as we have seen in previous chapters, one hundred and twenty-two German tanks arrived in Spain during the Spanish Civil War, and there were only thirty-eight "*negrillo*" *Panzer I* losses, i.e. 31% of the German tanks supplied. Counting the twenty-nine months (from

(Javier de Mazarrasa)

Top: once the war was over, the *Agrupación de Carros de La Legión* was gathered together in Madrid

Above and previous: Manoeuvres in 1940. The stars of the show were the *Panzer Is.* (Authors)

early November 1936 to late March 1939) they operated on the fronts, monthly losses reached a most acceptable figure of 1.31 *Panzer I* tanks per month.

The truth is, if we bear in mind the extremely poor performances of the German tank, along with the overwhelming Republican superiority in that class of weapons (BT-5, T-26 B, BA-6, Chevrolet M. 1937), one comes to the conclusion that either the Nationalist Army tank unit, with the support of the German instructors of the *Panzer Gruppe Drohne*, showed an exceptional behavior during the war, or the enemy, the Republican armored forces and anti-tank units, were really no match. In our opinion, it was neither the former nor the latter.

The behavior of the Nationalist tank units, equipped with "*negrillo*" tanks during the first months of the conflict, was rather modest, as the tank was intrinsically mediocre or really poor regarding classic mobility, protection, and firepower performance. But obviously equipment is not all. Disciplined and motivated units, with good training and high morale, and an optimal use of the resources available, apart from their capability to capture enemy equipment and reuse it themselves, was maybe the key to the success in that field during the war in Spain.

Top: 1940 Victory parade. The *Panzer Is* on parade on the American General Motors Company ACX-504 trucks. They belonged to *Regimiento de Carros de Combate n° 1*. (Cesar O'Donnell) Following page: Several vehicles of German origin march along the Avenida del Generalísimo in Madrid, a year after the end of the Spanish Civil War. (Cesar O'Donnell)

(Cesar O'Donnell)

The Republican armored forces were definitely an important enemy, because their 570 tanks, added to the nearly three hundred wheeled armored fighting vehicles, must not be disregarded. Certainly, the use of that armored mass was not the best, and probably not even good, but was undeniably an important enemy.

If a balance is to be made, we should categorically state that the Germans were much more stingy than the Russians as armored equipment supplies are regarded, but were much more right as regards the training of the Spanish personnel that were to man them. Besides,

Top and next page top: Impressive close-up of an American tank transport truck with a *Panzer I* on it. These vehicles were vital to take the tanks to the deployment area, thus preventing useless wear of the tank before they entered combat. (Cesar O'Donnell) Next page, bottom: One of the few *Panzerbefehlswagen* in Spain, on parade in the post-war. (Cesar O'Donnell)

A further two views of the panzers in the 1940 Victory parade. It is a pity that no complete specimen of the *Ausf.A* model is preserved in Spain. (Cesar O'Donnell)

In the foreground, a *Panzerkampfwagen I ohne aufbau* (without superstructure) from the training equipment of the *Panzer Gruppe Drohne* on parade in the post-war. Behind them, several T-26 modified in the same way. All of them were assigned to *Regimiento "Oviedo" nº 63*. (J. Mazarrasa)

the Germans became much less involved in combat than the Russians, nearly always acting as mere advisers and risking their men's lives very little (indeed, front casualties of the *Panzer Drohne* members are quite small).

The German heritage in the Spanish post-war tank units was obvious and, beside the black beret—which has persisted to the present—the doctrine and equipment remained well into the 1950s, when, after the signing of the agreements with the Americans and the arrival of armored equipment from that country, the last worn-out limping *Panzerkampfwagen Is* from the Civil War were phased out.

The mark of the German *Panzer Gruppe*, organized by that exceptional soldier Wilhelm *Ritter* von Thoma, was deep and lasting, and although it is possible that almost nobody in the Spanish tank units might remember it, the origin of the modern and agile armored units must be traced back to the German merchant vessels SS *Girgenti* and SS *Pasajes* that arrived in the port of Seville on 7 October 1936...

An excellent unpublished image showing two of the best-known panzer types. In the foreground, a *Panzerkampfwagen I Ausf. A* and a *Panzerkampfwagen IV Ausf. H* company behind, all of them belonging to *Regimiento de Carros de Combate "Alcázar de Toledo" nº 61*. (César O'Donnell)

10

Advisers for the *Falange Española*

Gruppe Issendorff

By mid-March 1937, the Generalissimo's HQs agreed to have a team of German officers that had been operating in Spain for a month and a half under *Obersteutnant* Walter von Issendorff's orders transferred to the *Falange Española de las JONS* Militia as instructors.

These German soldiers had arrived in Spain between late January and early February that same year, to take part in the military training of the junior officers of the militias that the *Falange* was organizing for the battlefronts.

The origins of this collaboration must be traced back to the ideological afinity—obviously, saving distances—between the *Falange Española de las JONS* and the German Nationalsocialists, besides the growing friendship between Manuel Hedilla, head of the *Junta de Mando Provisional* in the absence of José Antonio Primo de Rivera, and German ambassador Faupel, who, according to Hugh Thomas "...started to cultivate the Nazi spirit

September 1936. The Catalonian "Virgen de Monserrat" *Centuria* on training manoeuvres at Espinosa de los Monteros, Burgos, before joining the front. Second right is Carl von Haartman, the Finnish volunteer captain of the Nationalist Army who directed the *Mandos de Centuria* Academy at Pedro Llen, Salamanca. (via José Luis de Mesa)

Catalonian Falangists at Soncillo standing next to comrades of the Santander *Centuria*, with whom they lived the risks of the Spanish Civil War on the North front. (via Eduardo Veguillas)

among them...."—among Hedilla and his followers, of course. Indeed, in the last days of November 1936, after the recognition of Nationalist Spain by Italy and Germany, Hedilla negotiated with the German Embassy the dispatch of military instructors for the planned *Academias de Jefes de Centuria*.[16]

On 10 December, Faupel sent a note to his government specifying the request for these instructors, "...I thus beg, in the most urgent way, that the highest number possible of Spanish-speaking officers and warrant officers be sought (...). As a result of the ceaseless request from the top leader of the whole *Falange* (Manuel Hedilla) and in accordance with General Franco, I ask for the grant, above all, to detach *Maj* R. (sic) von Issendorff, from the Cavalry Inspection, to assume the direction of the training at the *Falange* academies all over Spain...."

By early 1937, Hedilla's secretary, Juan Serrallach Juliá, along with the Falangist Ramón Rico, took care of welcoming the German officers appointed by Berlin for the military training of his men.

After the numerous problems posed by the military authorities in Ávila, Toledo, and some other places, the C.G.G. sent an official letter to the commanders of the *Divisiones* 2ª, 5ª, 6ª, 7ª, and 8ª on 17 March, as well as to the Military Governor of Toledo, for the official communication of the authorization for these German officers to start their work. The official letter recommended that, as soon

Wilhelm Faupel, the first German Ambassador in Nationalist Spain. He was responsible for the posting of the German military instructors at the F.E. de las J.O.N.S. (via Raúl Arias)

as the German personnel reported to the authorities responsible, wherever they were to carry out their tasks, they be granted "...whatever facilities for the best carrying out of their tasks...."

The first *Academia de Jefes de Centuria* of *Falange* was established at the estate "La Jarilla," Seville, where the classes started as a boarding school during the first days of February. There were about fifty students of the Falangist party, with instructors of *1ª Línea de Falange Española*[17] and German military instructors who had just arrived in the peninsula by sea. *Oblt* Peter Bozung served as chief instructor with *Oblt* Joachim von Knobloch and three of the newcomer 1st lieutnenants. Only one class of *Jefes de Centuria de 1ª Línea* graduated at the academy, after a one-month course.

By early March the new *Academia Nacional de Jefes de Centuria* started up at Pedro Llen, an estate in Salamanca for the breeding of fighting bulls at Las Veguillas, about thirty kilometers from the province capital. By that same time, the Nationalist Militia HQs' Office took the decision to organize nine instructor teams to carry out similar tasks in the same number of towns in different provinces under the control of the rebels with these German officers. Specifically the province academies were in Toledo, Cadiz, Malaga, Soria, Palencia, Vitoria (Zuazo), Ávila, Cáceres, and Corunna, in the towns where these teams should move to train the Falangist students.

Command of these German volunteers, as pointed out above, was entrusted to a reserve Cavalry *Oberstleutnant* named Walter von Issendorff, with a Staff and the nine instructor teams mentioned above.

It was a total of forty-eight officers and three auxiliaries, many of them reservists, who were distributed among the teams and the Staff. These were joined in April by 1/Lt Oskar

Members of the Falangist militia forming up. The militia academies of the F.E. de las J.O.N.S. trained numerous *Centuria* COs for the units fighting on the front. (via Raúl Arias)

Dirlewanger, a somber character who, in the Second World War, was to command a strange and atypical *Waffen SS* Division.

The distribution and identity of its members were as follows:

GRUPPE ISSENDORFF COMPOSITION

Group CO	*Obstl.* Walther von Issendorff
Aide	*Lt.* Günther Albat
Staff	*Maj.* Rudolf Demme
	Hpt. Karl Steidinger
	Lt. (Paymastrr) Walter Finck
	Lt. Walter Leutner, Max Linz, Hermann Richter, Joachim von Winterfeld, Richard Wolf
	Aux. Hermann Roecker

Nine teams made up of a chief and three or four instructors, as follows:

TOWN	CHIEF INSTRUCTORS	INSTRUCTORS	ASSISTANT INSTRUCTORS	AUXILIARIES
Toledo	*Oblt.* Peter Bozung	*Oblt.* Otto Maxim Meyer		
		Lt. Kurt Schaefer		
		Lt. Richard Wolf		
Málaga	*Oblt.* Walter Haalck	*Oblt.* Karl Ganzenmueller		
		Lt. Stephan Straesser		
		Oblt. Johannes Gunz		
Cadiz	Hermann Hoefle*	*Oblt.* Joachim von Knobloch		Aloisius Mailly
		Lt Ernst Behrend		
		Oblt. Oscar Lohmueller		
Soria	*Maj.* August Martenstein	*Lt.* Heinz Ohlhorst	*Lt.* Alfred Lamprecht	
			Lt. Walter Freitag	Vitoria
	Maj. Frederick Herberg	*Lt.* Gerhard Poehl		
		Lt. Wilhelm Blume		
		Lt. Joachim Canaris		
Palencia	*Oblt.* Otto Fleiter	*Lt.* Victor Horn		
		Lt. Ludwig Lindemann	*Lt.* Jacob Becker	
Salamanca	*Oblt.* Johannes Baudach	*Lt.* Adolf Mueller		
		Lt. Vincent Fleiter		
		Lt. Arthur Schindler		
		Oblt. Eugen Hollmann		
Cáceres	*Maj.* Richard Holke	*Oblt.* Johannes Schmidt		Wilhelm Placke
		Kurt Otto**		
		Oblt. Heinrich Schuetz		
Corunna	*Oblt.* Frederich Koethke	*Oblt.* Felix Klumpp	*Lt.* Alfred Schlaterer	
		Lt. Johannes Mallet	Lt. Heinrich Schuetze	

* Hermann Hoefle's rank is not recorded here nor in the original listings of *Gruppe Thoma* (Academies), where all the other members of this group of instructors are mentioned. Probably he did not stay in Spain after the disbandment of the *Falange* academies.

** Nobody in the abovementioned personnel lists is recorded under that name. Maybe the same applies to the one above, and he may have returned to Germany in April 1937.

*** There is recorded evidence of the presence in Spain of another German called Herbert Kurka—fighting with the Falangists at El Alto del León, and later as an instructor in Valladolid. Not recorded here, though, nor later in the *Gruppe Thoma* (Academies) listings, it is quite probable that he returned to Germany before April.

The Unification Decree

Some tensions between different groups within José Antonio Primo de Rivera's beheaded and orphan *Falange*, which are irrelevant here, caused several incidents on 16 April. Hedilla had convened the National Council for that date so as to make it choose a new National Leader, by direct vote of its members. A triumvirate formed by Agustín Aznar, head of "*Primera Línea*," José Moreno, and Sancho Dávila, a cousin of José Antonio and head of the Andalusia *Falange*, all of whom opposed Hedilla, occupied—with several Falangists from Salamanca—the *Junta de Mando* (Command Junta) building in the town and decided to dismiss him. These events were observed with concern and tense calm from the Generalissimo's HQs in the town, and although some of its members like *teniente coronel* Barroso, and even Franco himself, met the fighting Falangist leaders, none of them sided with either of the warring factions, the *Caudillo* exhorting them to "...union and discipline...."

THE DARK FACE OF THE GERMAN INSTRUCTORS
OSKAR DIRLEWANGER

Oskar Dirlewanger was born on 26 September 1895 in Würzburg and joined the Army in 1913. He fought in the First World War in the 123 Infantry Regiment from the start. In 1915 he was promoted to 1st lieutenant; he was wounded several times in the conflict and was decorated with the 2nd and 1st Class Iron Cross, with really brilliant records as a whole.

As the war ended, he joined the *Freikorps* and later attended Frankfurt University, and became an Economy doctorate in 1922. He joined the NSDAP and enrolled in the SA that same year, taking part in the Munich Putsch along with the most important National Socialist leaders.

After Hitler's conquest of power Dirlewanger confronted the local Nazi authorities of Esslingen; he was expelled from the SA, and was accused of causing traffic accidents for drunkenness, as well as for maintaining immoral relationships with under-aged girls. For all that, he was sentenced to two years' prison. The NSDAP Wüttemberg-Hohenzollern Regional Leader, Wilhelm Murr, had sworn vengeance on him. However, he was backed by Gottlob Berger. In October 1936 he left the prison, but Murr sent him to a concentration camp until March 1937.

One month later, his friend Berger managed to have him sent to Spain as an instructor, where he was first posted to the *Tercio* and then to *Gruppe Issendorff*, until November 1937. Murr, in Germany, managed to have him arrested as "politically unreliable" and he was imprisoned in Toledo, from where some German police officers took him to Germany. However, his friend Berger and a positive report by von Thoma, who qualified him as a "good professional of the arms," had him back in Spain in July 1938. Von Thoma's report recorded him as company commander in training tasks and qualifies him as very remarkable.

After his return in Germany in May 1939 he applied for the SS, although he was rejected for his previous sentence. Inexplicably, he was admitted in 1940.

Manuel Hedilla, Head of the *Junta de Mando Provisional* of the F.E. de las J.O.N.S. (via Raúl Arias)

The truth is Hedilla did not accept his fate and, after ordering the local head of Salamanca, Ramón Laporta, to retake the headquarters, clearing everybody out, he urged the chief of the nearby *Academia de Mandos* at Pedro Llen, Finnish temporary Capt Carl von Haartman, to send a unit of Falangist cadets in order to achieve it. Laporta did not move; on the contrary, he put himself and his men—about 600—under Franco's orders; von Haartman demanded a written order from Hedilla. Shortly

Sancho Dávila, head of the Seville Falange and a cousin of José Antonio Primo de Rivera. (via Raúl Arias)

CARL VON HAARTMAN
A FINNISH ADVENTURER IN THE SPANISH CIVIL WAR

The director of the *Academia de Jefes de Centuria de F.E. de las J.O.N.S.* at Pedro Llen, Salamanca, was a 39-year-old Finnish Army captain called Carl Magnus Gunnar Emil von Haartman, an alledged relative of the hero of Finnish independence, Marshall Gustaf Mannerheim.

Born in Helsinki in 1897, he took an active part in the war for the independence of Finland in 1918. After the war, he was admitted as a cadet at the Air Military School established by the Germans in Libau, Latvia, but he did not graduate. In 1919 he entered the Finnish Military Academy and eventually graduated as a Cavalry first lieutenant. He was promoted to captain in 1921 and spent several years in Italy on commission. His adventurous character made him leave the Army and dragged him to America, where he arrived in 1924 and worked in Hollywood epics of the early cinema, such as Howard Hughes' "*Hell's Angels.*" He returned to Finland and continued his cinema career as an actor and director. In the mid-1930s he seemed to have lost interest in his job and life. Suddenly, in the summer of 1936, he decided to come and fight in Spain.

On 8 September 1936, after several adventures, he entered Spain to embrace the Nationalist cause and joined the *Milicias* de *Falange Española de las JONS* as an attached military instructor of the *1ª Centuria de la Territorial de Cataluña*. On 5 October he left for the Espinosa de los Monteros front with *teniente coronel* Moliner's column, took part in all the combats in that sector, and was wounded in the defense of "El Caballo" on 6 December. On 12 January 1937, after being appointed temporary Militia captain for the duration, he moved to Salamanca to assume the direction of the *Academia de Jefes de Centuria* of *Falange Española*.

For his support of Hedilla on 16 April 1937, when he sent all the students of the academy at Pedro Llen to Salamanca, von Haartman was arrested, although he was set free the following day under word of honor that he would not try to escape; he stayed at the Gran Hotel and remained inactive for several months.

On 6 June, German Ambassador Faupel asked after Captain Haartman, and asked the Generalissimo's Aide-de-Camp, Francisco Franco Salgado-Araujo, to let that soldier back to *teniente coronel* Moliner's column, where he had already served. The case was submitted to Franco, who decided that Haartman should indeed be attached to the column, where he continued fighting in the Nationalist Army. On 9 October, while he was commanding the *3º Batallón de FET de las JONS* de Burgos he was wounded on the Asturias front. Once recovered, he got back to his unit, where he was wounded again on 18 July 1938.

During the Second World War he fought in the Winter War and the Continuation War, and then was sent to Spain as Military Attaché. He lived and died in Malaga in 1980.

afterwards, Serrallach turned up at Pedro Llen with a signed order, and then Haartman obeyed and drove to Salamanca with fifty Falangist cadets, with whose help the *Junta de Mando* building was reoccupied that night.

That same night, after several rackets and shootings, two Falangists were killed—one of each rival faction—and the rest were arrested by *comandante* Doval's *guardias civiles*. The incidents and shootings had taken place a few yards from the Generalissimo's HQs, the leading body of the war that, lest we forget, raged on all fronts.

On the 18th, at the *Falange* III National Council meeting, Hedilla was chosen National Leader by ten votes to four and eight abstentions. That same night, Manuel Hedilla went to see Franco, who made a speech in his presence that was broadcast by *Radio Nacional de España*. He announced the unification of all parties and political groups of the Nationalist side in a single party, the *Falange Española Tradicionalista y de las JONS*.

The End of the *Falange* Academies

The last Falangist academy established (the official documents researched already mentioned the *Falange Española Tradicionalista y de las JONS*) was the one at Pinseque, Saragossa, which opened up 18 April 1937, one day before the Unification Decree was published in the *Boletín Oficial del Estado*.

Its chief instructor and, apparently, organizer was *Maj* Rudolf Demme, along with *Lt* Walter Leutner, Max Linz, and Hermann Richter and Joachim von Winterfeld as inspector, started it up along with a Spanish officer of the *5ª División*. On 7 May, twenty days after its foundation, this academy was closed down and the students were sent back to their original postings.

First right is Carl von Haartman, posing with several Spanish officers. (via Eduardo Veguillas)

In his masterly work on the temporary second lieutenants, Gárate Córdoba says:

"...It seems to be undoubted that the first German instructor officers arrived in Spain as an answer to the call from the *Falange* for the military training of their untrained *centuria* leaders to assume field command in campaign. It is still to be verified, although it seems to be certain, whether the forty instructors and auxiliaries in the list of the C.G.G. of 17 March 1937 for the nine province academies are those who later carried out the same mission at the temporary officers and sergeants academies. (...) Data regarding arrival in Spain, number and names of the possible lists are missing."

Well, from May 1937 on, all these instructors and those who arrived later were posted to the Infantry academies established by the *Jefatura de M.I.R.*

In the next chapter we shall answer the queries Gárate Córdoba posed regarding arrival data, number, and names of all the German instructors.

THE NATIONALIST *ACADEMIA DE JEFES DE CENTURIA* AT PEDRO LLEN

The first course in this academy started in early March 1937, with fifty students chosen for their records and called from the front, four per province. The classes taught included close order, use of arms, formation, parade, squad, section and company combat order, rifle firing and grenade launching, physical education, tactics, shooting, topography, and military regulations. It ended on 8 April; seven or eight of the brand new *Jefes de Centuria* stayed at the academy, without a posting, and these were claimed by Hedilla as instructors for future courses.

Once the first course ended, the students called for the second one were gathering at Pedro Llen, and the start date was scheduled for 12 April. It was attended by ninety students, although it was called off eight days later, after the bloody events of Salamanca and the participation of the young Falangists from Pedro Llen.

Rifle fire practice with members of the Falangist militia. The German instructors were at nine training schools of the Falange Española de las JONS. (via Raúl Arias)

11

Infantry Advisers: *Imker Ausbilder*
The Transformation of *Gruppe Issendorff*

The *Provisionales* academies

In order to judge the task of the German Army instructors in Spain in a way that is acceptably reasonable, it is first essential to summarize the significance of the huge and complex task of the training schools for temporary officers and NCOs.

Shortly after the start of the war, the need for junior officers (2nd lieutenants and 1s lieutenants), as well as lower rank NCOs (sergeants) became really pressing given the losses in these ranks, either because of the risks in combat or because they were "empowered" for higher ranks because of their experience or merits in campaign, and the growing needs involved by the constant increase of newly-born units to meet the demands of a large-scale war.

Thus, on 4 September 1936, it was the President of the *Junta de Defensa Nacional*, *general* Cabanellas, who laid the foundation stone of the huge construction that the training of temporary cadres was; the decision was published as Decree no 94 in the *Boletín Oficial del Estado* no 17, of 7 September. The idea to train officers to meet the pressing needs of the war had originated from *general* Mola and was approved by Franco, still not formally invested as Generalissimo at the moment. The provisional character, for the duration, in contrast with the complementary nature of the reserve officer corps, was the prevailing aspect of these new cadres.

As for officers, two schools were initially established in Burgos and Seville, followed shortly afterwards by others in Morocco and the Canary Islands. This organization, called "early period," was maintained from September 1936 to May 1937. In the first courses, length was fifteen working days, but was extended to twenty-four in January 1937. The instructors, except for those of the *Falange*, were always Spanish, basically retired or disabled veterans.

The school in Burgos, under the direction of retired Artillery *coronel* Félix Gil Verdejo, met the needs of the *Ejército del Norte*. Classes were initially given at the regimental academies of the artillery and infantry units based there. The first Infantry and Artillery Temporary 2nd lieutenants in all of Spain graduated there on 3 October. Later on, courses were also given for Cavalry at the *Regimiento de Lanceros de España* barracks, Engineers at Fuentes Blancas (two courses) and, at the end, Service Corps (one course). Classes were ven given in the Teatro Principal and the Teatro-Cine Avenida. Burgos also had branch chools in Palencia, Vitoria, and Luarca (Asturias) of ephemeral life and just for Infantry officers. In total, six courses were given there. The total number of officers that graduated vas 2,639.

Officers of the rest of the Nationalist Army units would train in Seville. There were a maximum of five courses of the four Arms and one for the Service Corps, with 1,460 officers graduated there.

Initially in Tetuán, but eventually in Xáuen, four courses were given for the Arms officers and one for the Service Corps. The latter, now in the spring of 1937, was given at Dar Riffien, in *La Legión* barracks, with a total of 749 prospective 2nd lieutenants.

Two courses were given in the Balearic Islands: the first one at the Monastery of the Palma de Mallorca mission, and the second one at the Monastery of Lluch, Escorca, with 200 students that graduated for the Infantry, Artillery, Engineers, and Service Corps. In the Canary Islands, the Infantry and Artillery school was established in Santa Cruz de Tenerife, with a total of 84 students that graduated as 1st lieutenants.

Enlistment oath of the 1 Course of Temporary Second Lieutenants Infantry in Ávila on 15 January 1938. (Authors)

Top: German instructor 1st lieutenant standing next to a Spanish student, firing a "ChauChat" automatic rifle, of those captured on board the SS *Silvia*. The Infantry academies got a large assortment of second-class armament not in very good condition. Bottom: fire practice with an automatic rifle of Soviet origin, Granada. (both Authors)

Toledo Infantry Academy. One of the W/O instructors from the *Gruppe Drohne* trains a temporary second lieutenant student on the use of the Luger P-08 pistol. (Authors)

The total figures of officers trained by all the schools was about 5,500 in round numbers, half of them in Burgos, with a monthly average output of about 640 officers. *Coronel* Gil Verdejo and his team were congratulated by Orders of 5 May 1937, published in the *Boletín Oficial del Estado* no 198, in the following words: "...With such a short single course, it is impossible to obtain better officers. (...) It is now a large number of those improvised officers who have died gallantly for Spain, thus honoring the Army and the Fatherland."

Besides, it was during the first phase of the establishment of the training schools for temporary officers that the ephemeral life of the *Milicias* academies, both those of the *Requeté*[18] and the *Falange*, went by.

Regarding the latter, we have already reviewed the operation of *Gruppe Issendorff*, operating in Spain since early February 1937, at the academies at La Jarilla (El Pedroso, Seville) first (only one course), at Pedro Llen (Salamanca) later, with another course, and at the province academies in Ávila, Cadiz, Cáceres, Corunna, Malaga, Palencia, Pinseque (Saragossa), Soria, Toledo, and Zuazo (Vitoria).

As regards that of the *Requeté*, one should be reminded that about 200 *carlista* "officers" had received military training in Mussolini's Italy, whereas others were trained at the *Academia Militar de Requetés* in Pamplona, established at the *Círculo Carlista* at Plaza del Castillo, and *general* Varela had organized the "units" from 1934 on, according to the *Ordenanzas del Requeté y Reglamento Táctico Requeté* (Regulations and Tactical Rules). In this context, it was intended to establish a *Real Academia de Estudios Militares de la Comunión Tradicionalista* or *Real Academia Militar de Requetés* de San Javier, by means of a *Real Decreto*[19] signed by Fal Conde, the Deputy Leader of the *Comunión Tradicionalista* on behalf of the Prince Regent, and published in the newspaper "*El Pensamiento Navarro*" on 16 December. The result of this action was the immediate invitation for Fal Conde either

Several Infantry W/O instructors closely inspect a T-2 B tank captured on the front. (J.M. Campesino via Rai

to expatriate himself, or to be court-martialled or treason charges, as the abovementioned "*Rea Decreto*" was clearly eroding the supreme authority of the hardly consolidated and unified, newly established Spanish state.

On 20 December 1936 all the militias on the Nationalist side were militarized and one month later, on 28 January 1937, it was determined that the militia volunteers would be allowed to attend the courses for temporary second lieutenants at the schools in Burgos, Seville, and Xáuen notwithstanding the number of places available, i.e. as an addition to the places officially announced.

The second period of the training of temporary officers started with the establishment of the *Servicios de Movilización, Recuperación y Preparación e Instrucción* of the Officer corps at the Rearguard Academies, later known as *Movilización, Instrucción y Recuperación* (*M.I.R*), and the appointment of *general de división* Luis Orgaz Yoldi at its head, which took place on 25 March 1937. This most notable body, which brought together the current equivalent of the Personnel and Logistic Support Commands, was of supreme importance for the Nationalist side's success during the war. Their task deserves recognition that, in general, it has never received, either then or in the present.

General de división Luis Orgaz Yoldi, appointed Head of *Movilización, Instrucción y Recuperación* in March 1937. (Authors)

Practice class at the Temporary Sargents Academy in Vitoria. In this case, the trainees watch the operation of smoke canisters. (J.M. Campesino via Raúl Arias)

Coronel Gil Verdejo, the founder of the first one in Burgos, joined the Staff as *Jefe de la Sección de Instrucción e Inspector de Academias*.

By early May, *general* Orgaz had already drawn up the reorganized training system, which involved the disbandment of the old schools and the establishment of new academies, using the experience and instructors of the former, at least in part. It was based on a more intensive modern training, as a board school and with the use of German and Italian instructors. As a requirement for candidates, they had to be high school graduates. Length of the courses was initially twenty-four working days, which soon extended to thirty and, by early 1938, to two months.

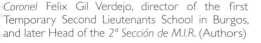

Coronel Felix Gil Verdejo, director of the first Temporary Second Lieutenants School in Burgos, and later Head of the *2ª Sección de M.I.R.* (Authors)

Commanded by a colonel, and mainly with Spanish instructors—selected retired disabled, and wounded or convalescent—the following Infantry Academies were established:

- Fuencaliente (at Miranda de Ebro, Burgos), for the *Ejército del Norte*, later moved in January 1938 to Ávila, where it stayed till the end of the war.
- Granada, for the *Ejército del Centro* (Center Army).
- Riffien (Morocco), for the *Ejército del Sur*, supplemented with that at Tauima for temporary captains.

Later, in November 1938, the one in Pamplona joined the system and, in an intermittent way, so did the old one at Lluch, in the Balearic Islands.

When it was decided to train officers for the mixed Spanish-Italian "legionnaire" units, the corresponding academy was established at Dueñas, Palencia, later to be moved to Medina del Campo, Valladolid.

The *Academia* in Toledo, initially established for the training of 2nd lieutenants, after just one month as such became the "*Academia de Ampliación y Perfeccionamiento*" for Infantry officers.

A total of some 18,000 Infantry 2nd lieutenants graduated there in the period.

The German instructors became integrated in most of these schools, with tasks ranging from training to the execution of tactical exercises. This included a major, an aide 1st lieutenant, and some warrant officers in the staff, and one or two officers with a warrant officer per company.

There were also Italian instructors at the temporary officers academies, for, as soon as the CTV HQs heard of the German contribution, they managed to get the approval, by early June, of a *Centro Italiano para Adiestramiento de Oficiales Españoles* (CIAUS)[20] attached to the *M.I.R* Staff. In order to prevent likely interferences and conflicts with the Germans, training areas were defined, the Italians taking part at those of the Artillery, Cavalry, and

Temporary Sergeants Academy in Vitoria. Practice exercise of hand grenade launching. (J.M. Campesino via Raúl Arias)

Engineers and, of course, the abovementioned ones at Dueñas and Medina del Campo.

The total number of "temporary" officers promoted to the ranks of 2nd lieutenant and 1st lieutenant was nearly 29,000 as a whole in the three war years.

Solutions similar to those implemented with officers were brought together for sergeants, based on Decree no 50 of the *Junta de Defensa Nacional*, dated 18 August 1936, by means of which corporals, sergeants, and NCOs of the Arms, Corps, and Services were promoted to the next rank. Later, on 30 April 1937, after the establishment of the *M.I.R*, the *Academias de Formación de Sargentos Provisionales* were established.

German instructor captain of the Toledo Infantry Academy, teaching theory on the *Stielhandgrenate*, or stick hand grenade of German origin. (Authors)

The Infantry academies were at Tafalla, Pamplona, in order to meet the needs of the *Cuerpos de Ejército* 5°, 6°, and 8° (Army Corps), at Plasencia, Cáceres, those of the 7°, and at San Roque, Cádiz, those of the *Ejército del Sur*. Given the constant demand caused by endless casualty rates, these were soon joined by those at Jerez de la Frontera, Fuencaliente, Riffien, Soria, Lluch and Dueñas, and Cigales, Valladolid, for the "*Unidades Legionarias*," or "*Flechas*" divisions.

The total numbers of temporary sergeants trained in such a short time frame reached an impressive 24,500; in round numbers, only slightly smaller than those for 2nd lieutenants.

In order to assess the task of the German instructors, with the background of the general overview seen above, the chart below, so far unpublished, was established by the authors on the bases of different documents traced at the *Archivo General Militar de Ávila*:

Spanish personnel trained by Germans at Infantry academies, 1 May 1937 - 1 May 1939

Academy	Courses	Students
Oficiales, Toledo	15	4,595
Alféreces, Fuentecaliente	4	1,412
Alféreces y Tenientes, Ávila	17	3,744
Alféreces, Granada	20	6,324
Oficiales, Pamplona	8	1,753
Oficiales, Jerez de la Frontera	1	224
Sargentos, Tafalla	4	1,808
Sargentos, Jerez de la Frontera	6	2,639
Sargentos, San Roque	16	7,643
Sargentos, Vitoria	10	3,846
Sargentos, Soria	3	641
Sargentos, Plasencia	1	423
Sargentos, Fuentecaliente	6	1,856
Sargentos de Automóviles	4	670
Total personnel trained		37,578

These documents, found among those sent to the Archive in recent dates from the former *Ministerio del Ejército*, include a report from the *Jefatura de M.I.R.* regarding German participation in the training of temporary officers and NCOs, which—because of its interest—is reproduced below:

"...When the *Jefatura de M.I.R.* was established, it absorbed the '*negrillo*' teams that were training the *Falange* Units and annexed them as part of the Infantry academies. Those teams were under the command of Lieutenant Colonel Von Issendorff. In parallel, there was the *Grupo Thoma*, commanded by Colonel Von Thoma, who was in charge of the '*negrilla*' collaboration at the Specialty academies, such as tanks, antitank guns, mine throwers, etc. where this Section did not participate. Colonel Von Thoma was the head of all the '*negrillo*' teams. Both field officers have taken part in the drawing up of the Circumstantial Technical Directives and have presented a series of initiatives and works for the improvement of training at the Military Academies. In November 1937, Lieutenant Colonel Von Issendorff was relieved by Colonel Knoerzer and both Groups merged about two months ago under the leadership of Colonel Von Thoma.

Relationships between the '*negrillo*' teams and the academies' personnel has been one of the issues of greatest concern for the Section. Regulations have often been issued to regulate the relations and the living together with the '*negrillos*,' which has brought success in the collaboration. These '*negrillo*' teams have supplied this HQs Office with abundant German professional literature and with a series of German rule books that are currently at the Section Library, and some of them have been translated. An Artillery Training Group has been operating for some time at Monasterio de Rodilla under the orders of *comandante* Antonio Lucena and under the inspection of Artillery Colonel Lucht, with German equipment and instructors.

They have also taken part in the training courses for Automobile sergeants and *Infantería de Marina*[21] second lieutenants.

They have always proved an extreme interest in having the academies supplied with good equipment and armament, and have provided them with materiel and armament of their own...."

It is clear from the communiqué from the *Jefatura de M.I.R.* that, besides the instructors at the Infantry academies, there were other Germans at the artillery, sappers, signals, mine throwers, chemical warfare, and automobile

A German instructor taking part in the training and use of Valero mortars (Infantry collective weapons) at the *provisionales* Academy in Ávila. (Authors)

Top: Several German instructor officers in friendly conversation with a Protectorate VIP during a military parade. (J.M. Campesino via Raúl Arias) Bottom: The German instructors of the Temporary Sergeants Academy at San Roque, marching past the civil and military authorities and the public. La Línea de la Concepción, Cadiz, 26 February 1938. (via Raúl Arias)

training tasks, and even at the *Escuela Naval* at San Fernando. All of them will be reviewed in the following chapters of this book.

Armament and Equipment in the Infantry Academies

Since the establishment of the Infantry academies in May 1938, different sorts of armament—second class all of it as far as their performances, condition, and age were concerned—such as magazine rifles and sub-machineguns captured from the enemy were being used in the training of the students, for which reason training lacked the minimum of teaching that could ensure the knowledge and use of the most efficient weapons in infantry combat.

The *"negrillo"* teams, and their commander, Wilhelm von Thoma, had announced the *Jefatura de M.I.R.* the arrival of different modern Infantry armament from Germany for the academies where they were collaborating, and could achieve the best results proportional to the efforts and the tenacity devoted to their training task. Indeed, in a letter sent by Colonel von Thoma to *general* Orgaz on 30 May 1938, among other things he said:

"...Training becomes often difficult for the lack of suitable weapons and theory does not achieve the practice that is necessary on the field..."

It was the German commander himself who negotiated the acquisition of the necessary armament from his country, which arrived by early June 1938 and was next distributed by the *Jefatura de M.I.R.* itself as shown in the following list:

Armament, ammunition and equipment acquired from Germany for the Infantry academies*

Equipment	Toledo	Ávila	Granada	Jerez	San Roque	Vitoria
Kar 98 carbines	300	600	600	500	500	500
Bayonet-Machetes	300	600	600	500	500	500
Shovels and shovel holders	300	600	600	500	500	500
Submachine guns	30	30	30	20	20	19
Signal pistols	25	18	18	18	18	18
Drill cartridges	1,500	3,000	3,000	2,500	2,500	2,500
Blank cartridges	34,000	54,000	54,000	36,000	36,000	36,000
Smoke canisters	2,400	3,000	3,000	1,800	1,800	1,800
Grenades	2,400	3,000	3,000	1,800	1,800	1,800
Field telephones	2	2	2	2	2	2
Range finders	1	-	1	-	1	1

* Only the most important German equipment for the Infantry academies is listed here

Enlistment oath of the Temporary Sergeants Academy at San Roque. In the foreground is one of the instructors from the *Drohne*. (National Library)

The German Advisers

The structure of the temporary officer and NCO academies themselves, as well as those for upper training, did not allow for the availability of the number of teachers and instructors necessary in full swing, for the high command made use of retired, disabled, war convalescent officers, etc. for this purpose; this problem was much more serious at the Infantry academies because of the handicap that this Spanish personnel was not fit enough to teach rehearsal and training exercises, which required younger, tough personnel.

This serious handicap was solved after several agreements with the Germans in Spain were reached to obtain the collaboration of *"negrillo"* instructors, by using those from the disbanded *Falange Española* schools, reinforced by newly-arrived German soldiers and supplemented by instructors chosen among the former students that had graduated at the academies themselves.

At each Infantry academy where the Germans were assigned there was a Team Chief, normally a lieutenant colonel— although sometimes this might be a major or even a captain— several company (captain or lieutenant) and section (1st lieutenant or 2nd lieutenant) COs, as well as different instructors, who were often warrant officers or sergeants. Rotation was continuous, with very few cases of German instructors that stayed at the same academy for their entire stay in Spain. In order to corroborate this statement, a most interesting

The colonel head of the Infantry Temporary Second Lieutenants Academy in Granada, in friendly conversation with the German chief instructor of the academy. (Authors)

document from the Academy for Infantry temporary second lieutenants in Pamplona, dated 14 March 1939, is excerpted next, listing the "Chiefs, Captains and Lieutenants of the '*Cóndor*' Instructor Team with a statement of the courses they have taught each since the establishment of the Academy":

TEMPORARY SECOND LIEUTENANTS ACADEMY, PAMPLONA

Rank	Name	Courses given
Lt Col	Heinert, Helmuth	2nd
Lt Col	Demme, Rudolf	$6^{th}, 7^{th}$, and 8th
Maj	Abelain, Theodor	5th and 6th
Capt	Bozung, Peter	1st and 4th
Capt	Hoffman, Hermann	4th
Capt	Bunckardt, Walter	5th
Capt	Steidinger, Karl	$5^{th}, 6^{th}, 7^{th}$, and 8th
Capt	Ganzemüller, Karl	$6^{th}, 7^{th}$, and 8th
Lt	Mallet, Johannes	1st and 2nd
Lt	Schultz, Heinrich	2nd
Lt	Fleiter, Vincenz	2nd
Lt	Mueller, Adolf	2nd
Lt	Linz, Max	4th
Lt	Stenzel, Hans	4th
Lt	Lohmueller, Oscar	4th
Lt	von Winterfeld, Joachim	4th and 6th
Lt	Horn, Victor	$6^{th}, 7^{th}$, and 8th

Enlistment oath of the Temporary Sergeants at the Vitoria Academy on 26 June 1937. (J.M. Campesino via Raúl Arias)

On 1 May 1937, the official starting date for the second phase of the training of temporary 2nd lieutenants and sergeants and perfectioning of Infantry officers, *general* Orgaz had ninety-four German instructors at the different academies of the corps for training tasks, fifty-four of whom were former instructors of the *Falange Española* Militia, commanded by *Oberstleutnant* Walter von Issendorff, and forty were supplied for the task by Colonel Wilhelm *Ritter* von Thoma from his tank units. During the remainder of 1937, one hundred and thirteen German instructors arrived in Spain for the Infantry academies, and a total of thirty-nine were stuck off charge.

By the end of 1937, there were one hundred and sixty-eight German instructors in Spain at the different Infantry academies for temporary officers and sergeants.

During 1938, another fifty-four Germans arrived in Spain and another fifty-eight died or returned to Germany, so the total number of those present in Spain on 31 December 1938 was one hundred and sixty-four men.

Finally, another five instructors arrived in Spain and eleven left until May 1939, for which reason, when the *Legión Cóndor* left for Germany on 26 May 1939, there were one hundred and fifty-eight Infantry instructors that boarded the *Wilhelm Gustlof* for the Reich.

Infantry Instructor changes			
Period	Joined	Left	Total
05/37-12/37	207	39	168
01/38-12/38	54	58	164
01/39-05/39	5	11	158

Fraternal meal on 26 June 1937, after the enlistment oath of the Temporary Sergeants of the Vitoria Academy. In the background are the Academy field officers and the German instructors. (J.M. Campesino via Raúl Arias)

The German Advisers' Uniforms

The *Gruppe Issendorff* members, i.e. of the *Imker Ausbilder*, basically used to wear th same uniforms as the rest of the *Legión Cóndor* members. A large part of the instructors mainly the officers, were German reserve personnel, although others came from operationa military units. All of them wore the rank badges (stars or gallons) on the chest, like all the German soldiers in Spain did, but many used to wear them on a rectangle—white fo the infantry, red for the artillery, or black for the engineers—which they sewed on thei uniforms and was easily recognizable in the distance.

As we saw when reviewing the *Panzer Gruppe Drohne* members, beside the oper tunic, brown shirt, and black tie, the German instructors—Infantry, Artillery, Sappers, o Signals—used to wear their breeches and high boots or long straight trousers and shoes ir their own way.

(J.M. Campesino via Raúl Arias)

MEMBERS OF THE "GROUP THOMA INFANTRY-ACADEMIES"

NAME	RANK	INSTRUCTOR	REMARKS
Abelein, Teodor	Maj	11/38-05/39	Chief Instructor Vitoria Academy
Albat*, Günther	1/Lt	05/37-03/38	Coy CO. Aide to Lt Col von Issendorff
Baudach*, Johann	Capt	05/37-06/38	Chief Instructor Vitoria Academy
Becker*, Jacob	1/Lt	05/37-05/39	Section & Coy CO
Behrend*	Ernst	1/Lt	05/37-05/37 Returned Germany 18/05/37
Benner, Ricardo	2/Lt	09/37-04/38	Section CO
Blume*, Wilhelm	1/Lt	05/37-06/37	Coy CO. Killed 01/07/37
Bozung*, Peter	Capt	05/37-05/39	Coy CO & Chief Instructor Pamplona Academy
Canaris*, Joachim	1/Lt	05/37-05/39	Coy CO
Clauss Kindt, Adolfo	Capt	10/36-05/39	von Thoma's interpreter
Demme*, Rudolf	Lt Col	05/37-05/39	Chief Instructor Pamplona Academy
Dirlewanger*, Oscar	1/Lt	05-10/37 & 08/38-05/39	Section & Coy CO
Fechner, Kurt	1/Lt	09/37-05/39	Section & Coy CO
Finck*, Walter	1/Lt	05/37-05/39	Paymaster 1/Lt
Fleiter*, Oton	Capt	05/37-05/39	Coy CO
Fleiter*, Vincenz	1/Lt	05/37-05/39	Section & Coy CO
Freitag*, Walter	1/Lt	05/37-05/39	Section & Coy CO
Ganzenmueller*, Carl	Capt	05/37-05/39	Coy CO
Grosse*, Erich	Col	05/37-05/39	Chief Instructor Toledo Academy
Gunz*, Johannes	Capt	05/37-05/39	Coy CO
Haalck*, Walter	Capt	05/37-08/37	Coy CO
Heinert, Helmuth	Lt Col	11/37-11/38	Chief Instructor Ávila Academy
Herberg*, Frederick	Lt Col	05/37-05/39	Chief Instructor Granada Academy
Hoffmann, Hermann	Lt Col	01/37-05/39	Chief Instructor San Roque Academy
Hoffmann, Johann	1/Lt	11/37-01/39	Coy CO
Holke*, Ricardo	Lt Col	05/37-05/39	Chief Instructor Ávila Academy
Hollmann*, Eugen	Capt	05/37-04/38	Coy CO
Horn*, Victor	1/Lt	05/37-05/39	Coy CO
von Issendorff*, Walter	Lt Col	05/37-11/37	Academies Chief Instructor
Jauckens, Ricardo	Auxiliary	05/37-05/39	Interpreter 10/36 05/37
Klumpp*, Felix	Capt	05/37-05/39	Coy CO
Knieling, Otto	1/Lt	08/38-03/39	Coy CO
Von Knobloch*, Hans-J.	Capt	05/37-05/39	Coy CO
Knoerzer, Johann	Col	08/37-12/38	Academies Chief Instructor
Koethke*, Frederick	Capt	05/37-07/37	Coy CO
Lamprecht*, Alfred	1/Lt	05/37-05/39	Section & Coy CO
Leutner*, Walter	1/Lt	05/37-05/39	Staff
Lindemann*, Ludwig	1/Lt	05/37-05/39	Section & Coy CO
Linz*, Max	1/Lt	05/37-05/39	Coy CO
Lohmüller*, Oskar	Capt	05/37-05/39	Coy CO
Mailly*, Aloisius	Auxiliary	05/37-05/39	Auxiliary
Mallet*, Johann	1/Lt	05/37-05/39	Coy CO
Martenstein*, August	Lt Col	05/37-05/39	Chief Instructor Soria Academy
Meyer-Thor S.*, Otto Max	Capt	05/37-05/39	Coy CO
Mueller*, Adolf	1/Lt	05/37-05/39	Coy CO
Ohlhorst*, Heinz	1/Lt	05/37-05/39	Coy CO. Killed 15/05/1937
Placke*, Wilhelm	1/Lt	05/37-05/39	Section & Coy CO
Poehl*, Gerard	1/Lt	05/37-05/39	Section & Coy CO
Richter, Hermann	1/Lt	05/37-05/39	Section & Coy CO
Roecker*, Hermann	Auxiliary	05/37-10/37	Auxiliary

Rose, Erich	1/Lt	06/37-08/38	Coy CO. Transferred to *Legión Española*
Rueggeberg, Karl Heinrich	1/Lt	01/38-05/39	Colonel von Funck's orderly officer
Schaefer*, Kurt	1/Lt	05/37-06/37	Coy CO
Schaer, Ernst	Lt Col	09/37-06/38	Chief Instructor Ávila Academy
Schindler*, Arthur	1/Lt	05/37-08/37	Section & Coy CO
Schlatterer*, Alfred	1/Lt	05/37-05/39	Section & Coy CO
Schmidt*, Johann	Capt	05/37-05/39	Coy CO
Schuetz*, Heinrich	Capt	05/37-05/39	Coy CO
Schuetze*, Heinrich	1/Lt	05/37-11/38	Section & Coy CO
Steidinger*, Carl	Capt	05/37-05/39	Coy CO
Stenzel*, Johannes	1/Lt	05/37-05/39	Coy CO
Straesser*, Esteban	1/Lt	05/37-05/39	Coy CO
von Winterfeld*, Joachim	1/Lt	05/37-05/39	Coy CO
Wolf*, Ricardo	1/Lt	05/37-08/37	Coy CO (Killed 01/08/37)
Wolff, Erwin	Lt Col	05/37-05/39	Chief Miranda Academy. 12/36-05/37, interpreter

These are the sixty-five men who are listed under the heading *"GRUPO THOMA-ACADEMIAS"* in the *Gruppe Imker* official documents, and were posted at some of the Infantry Academies. The list includes the *Falange* instructors mentioned in the previous chapter, for practically all of them joined the Infantry academies for temporary 2nd lieutenants and sergeants as instructors for a shorter or longer period.

All the instructors from the *Falange* academies are listed with an asterisk. Their stay in Spain is only recorded as of May 1937, when they served as Infantry instructors.

MEMBERS OF THE *IMKER AUSBILDER*, INFANTRY INSTRUCTORS

NAME	RANK	INSTRUCTOR	REMARKS
Armbruster, Frederik	2/Lt	06-37 / 05-39	Section CO
Baaske, Adolf	W/O	12-37 / 07-38	Instructor
Bahlert, Walter	W/O	06-37 / 05-39	Instructor
Baldzuhn, Kurt	W/O	11-38 / 05-39	Instructor
Baron, Hermann	W/O	12-37 / 08-38	Instructor
Becker, Hermann	W/O	12-37 / 05-39	Instructor
Bender, Paul	W/O	12-37 / 12-38	Instructor
Bennemann, Karl	2/Lt	09-38 / 05-39	Instructor
Berthold, Kurt	2/Lt	11-37 / 09-38	Section CO
Blask, Kurt	W/O	11-38 / 05-39	Instructor
Bloeck, Heribert	W/O	11-38 / 05-39	Instructor
Blum, Alfred	W/O	11-38 / 05-39	Instructor
Bocksch, Gerard	2/Lt	11-37 / 11-38	Section CO
Boettcher, Ernst	2/Lt	11-38 / 05-39	Instructor
Bosselmann, Kurt	2/Lt	08-38 / 07-04-39	Section CO (killed in accident)
Braeutigam, Johann	W/O	06-37 / 12-38	Instructor
Brandt, Paul	2/Lt	08-38 / 05-39	Section CO
Breitkopf, Rudolf	2/Lt	11-37 / 12-38	Section CO
Bruechner, Philip	2/Lt	11-37 / 05-39	Section CO
Brun, Arthur	2/Lt	08-38 / 05-39	Section CO

NAME	RANK	INSTRUCTOR	REMARKS
Burckhardt, Walter	Capt	08-37 / 12-38	Academy Chief Instructor
Demmler, Alfred	2/Lt	11-37 / 05-39	Section CO
Deusser, Karl	W/O	12-37 / 09-38	Instructor
Dickel, Ewald	W/O	06-37 / 05-39	Instructor
Dost, Gustav	2/Lt	11-38 / 05-39	Instructor
Dubbert, Robert	W/O	11-38 / 31-05-39	Instructor
Fleischer, Otto	W/O	06-37 / 12-38	Instructor
Frank, Arno	2/Lt	06-37 / 02-38	Section CO
Funck, Richard	2/Lt	01-38 / 09-38	Section CO
Gabriel, Alfred	W/O	06-37 / 05-39	Section CO
Garling, Otto	2/Lt	12-38 / 05-39	Section CO
Gebhardt, Johann	2/Lt	11-37 / 05-39	Section CO
Gerlach, Juergen	Capt	11-38 / 05-39	Coy CO
Goennawein, Helmuth	W/O	06-37 / 05-39	Instructor
Grandel, Günther	W/O	11-37 / 05-39	Instructor
Greulich, Frederik	W/O	12-37 / 11-38	Instructor
Gross, Philip	Maj	11-38 / 05-39	Section CO
Gruendel, Gerard	W/O	11-37 / 05-39	Instructor
Hahmann, Robert	Capt	11-38 / 01-39	Coy CO
Haisch, Alfred	2/Lt	12-37 / 05-39	Section CO
Hantelmann, Wilhelm	1/Lt	11-37 / 11-38	Coy CO
Hardt, Jurgen	2/Lt	08-38 / 07-04-39	Section CO (killed in accident)
Haushalter, Otto	W/O	11-38 / 05-39	Instructor
Hermann, Walter	2/Lt	03-39 / 05-39	Instructor
Hess, Richard	W/O	11-37 / 09-38	Instructor
Hettinger, Heinrich	W/O	06-37 / 11-38	Instructor
Heuer, Gerard	W/O	12-37 / 05-39	Instructor
Heynitz, Max	2/Lt	11-37 / 05-38	Section CO
Hilgers, Hermann	W/O	12-37 / 05-39	Instructor
Hinners, Heinrich	W/O	06-37 / 01-38	Instructor (died January 1938)
Hirschfelder, Kurt	2/Lt	06-37 / 05-39	Section CO
Hoeding, Ewald	2/Lt	08-38 / 05-39	Section CO
Hoeinghaus, Godofred	2/Lt	12-37 / 12-38	Section CO
Hoeweler, Heinrich	2/Lt	11-38 / 05-39	Section CO
Hoffmeister, Hermann	W/O	12-37 / 12-38	Instructor
von Huelsen, Wolf	Maj	08-37 / 08-38	Academy Chief Instructor
Jansen, Johann	W/O	06-37 / 12-38	Instructor
Jaworowski, Paul	2/Lt	08-38 / 05-39	Section CO
Kallas, Paul	W/O	11-38 / 05-39	Instructor
Kambersky, Heinrich	2/Lt	11-37 / 05-39	Section CO
Kammann, Bernard	Capt	11-37 / 02-39	Academy Chief Instructor
Karutz, Paul	W/O	11-38 / 05-39	Instructor
Kautzmann, Karl	W/O	12-37 / 05-39	Instructor
Kempf, Robert	2/Lt	12-37 / 05-39	Section CO
Kiesgen, Peter	W/O	11-38 / 05-39	Instructor
Klauss, Wilhelm	2/Lt	11-37 / 09-38	Section CO
Klemm, Frederik G.	1/Lt	11-38 / 05-39	Section CO
Koss, Arthur	W/O	11-38 / 05-39	Instructor
Kott, Heinrich	Maj	11-37 / 11-38	Academy Chief Instructor
Kraehahn, Werner	W/O	11-37 / 05-39	Instructor
van Kranenbrock, Wolfgang	2/Lt	11-37 / 08-38	Section CO
Kroll, Hugo	2/Lt	06-37 / 05-39	Section CO
Kummer, Albert	2/Lt	06-37 / 05-39	Section CO

NAME	RANK	INSTRUCTOR	REMARKS
Kumpel, Claus	W/O	11-38 / 05-39	Instructor
Kunzmann, Otto	2/Lt	03-39 / 05-39	Instructor
Kura, Erich	2/Lt	11-37 / 08-38	Section CO
Lemke, Ferdinand	W/O	06-37 / 12-38	Instructor
Littwin, Alfons	2/Lt	07-38 / 05-39	Section CO
Lohr, Erich	2/Lt	11-37 / 09-38	Section CO
Lukas, Heinrich	W/O	11-38 / 05-39	Instructor
Lux, Walter	2/Lt	08-38 / I05-39	Section CO
Maetzing, Heinrich	W/O	11-38 / 05-39	Instructor
Maier, Fridolin	Capt	08-38 / 05-39	Coy CO
Meier, Werner	2/Lt	11-38 / 05-39	Section CO
Meierkordt, Heribert	2/Lt	12-37 / 12-38	Section CO
Menke, Louis	W/O	12-37 / 03-39	Instructor
Mentnich, Karl	W/O	06-37 / 05-39	Instructor
Menzer, Karl	2/Lt	06-37 / 05-39	Section CO
Mindt, Peter	W/O	06-37 / 12-38	Instructor
Mittelstorb, Heinrich	2/Lt	06-37 / 07-04-39	Section CO (killed in accident)
Mohr, Michael	W/O	12-37 / 05-39	Instructor
Monte, Georg	W/O	06-37 / 05-38	Instructor
Mueller, Karl	W/O	06-37 / 05-39	Instructor
Muenster, Reinald	W/O	12-37 / 05-39	Instructor
Muth, Hugo	W/O	11-37 / 05-39	Instructor
Neeb, Andreas	W/O	11-38 / 05-39	Instructor
Neumann, Erich	W/O	11-37 / 12-38	Instructor
Niemann, Wolfgang	1/Lt	11-38 / 05-39	Section CO
Nowakowski, Ernst	2/Lt	11-37 / 03-39	Section CO
Ohle, Karl	2/Lt	08-38 / 12-38	Section CO
Otto, Adolf	W/O	03-39 / 05-39	Instructor
Perker, Erich	1/Lt	11-38 / 05-39	Section CO
Pinckert, Gerhardt	1/Lt	11-38 / 05-39	Section CO
Prael, Rudolf	Capt	07-38 / 05-39	Coy CO
Proels, Jurgen	W/O	06-37 / 05-38	Instructor
Raehse, Kurt	2/Lt	03-39 / 05-39	Instructor
Roese, Otto	2/Lt	08-38 / 05-39	Section CO
Rossnagel, Philipp	2/Lt	11-38 / 05-39	Section CO
Rupp, Alexander	2/Lt	08-38 / 05-39	Section CO
Rybka, Frank	2/Lt	07-38 / 05-39	Section CO
Schachler, Joseph	W/O	11-37 / 05-39	Instructor
Schaumburg, Walter	W/O	06-37 / 24-07-37	Instructor (killed in accident)
Schlueter, Wilhelm	2/Lt	06-37 / 05-38	Section CO
Schmarbeck, Gerhard	2/Lt	08-38 / 05-39	Section CO
Schmidt, Albert	W/O	06-37 / 05-39	Instructor
Schmidt, Frederik	2/Lt	02-38 / 05-39	Section CO
Schmidt, Walter	2/Lt	08-38 / 05-39	Section CO
Schoenfeld, Erich	2/Lt	11-37 / 12-38	Section CO
Schubert, Günther	2/Lt	11-37 / 05-39	Section CO
Schulze, Otto	W/O	06-37 / 05-39	Instructor
Schumacher, Gerhard	W/O	11-37 / 09-38	Instructor
von Schweinitz, Frederich	1/Lt	11-37 / 05-39	Coy CO
Sedlmair, Wolfgang	2/Lt	12-37 / 05-39	Section CO
Seip, Philip	W/O	06-37 / 02-38	Instructor
Spier, Wilhelm	W/O	12-37 / 05-39	Instructor

AME	RANK	INSTRUCTOR	REMARKS
pranger, Rudolf	2/Lt	11-37 / 07-04-39	Section CO (killed in car crash)
trobelt, Sigfried	W/O	06-37 / 03-39	Instructor
rutz, Walter	2/Lt	11-38 / 05-39	Section CO
uewe, Wilhelm	2/Lt	06-37 / 03-38	Section CO
uewe, Kurt	W/O	03-39 / 05-39	Instructor
eubner, Martin	2/Lt	11-37 / 12-38	Section CO
hielecke, Heribert	2/Lt	11-38 / 05-39	Section CO
rautnitz, Johann	W/O	11-37 / 11-38	Instructor
raxel, Rudolf	2/Lt	06-37 / 05-39	Section CO
schiersch, Alfons	2/Lt	11-37 / 07-38	Section CO
Valther, Harald	Capt	11-37 / 11-38	Coy CO
Vanzek, Ewald	2/Lt	03-39 / 05-39	Instructor
Venzel, Walter	W/O	11-37 / 12-38	Instructor
Vessel, Wilhelm	2/Lt	11-37 / 08-38	Section CO
Vichterich, Frank	W/O	06-37 / 05-39	Instructor
Vindisch, Kurt	W/O	11-38 / 05-39	Instructor
Vinkler, Erich	2/Lt	11-37 / 05-38	Section CO
Vinkler, Johannes	1/Lt	11-38 / 05-39	Coy CO
Voelfl, Joseph	2/Lt	12-37 / 05-39	Section CO
Vuesthof, Gerhard	2/Lt	11-37 / 05-38	Section CO
uelsdorf, Günther	W/O	11-37 / 09-38	Instructor

(Authors)

The *Gruppe Issendorff* (Infantry) Casualties

Nine Infantry instructors were killed/died during the Spanish Civil War: one of them in a training accident; four in a truck crash in the province of Burgos; and three died of illness caught in Spain and one of sudden death to natural causes upon arrival in Germany.

NAME	RANK	DATE	CAUSE & PLACE
Blume, Wilhelm	Lt	01-07-1937	Sudden death upon arrival, Germany
Bosselmann, Kurt	2/Lt	07-04-1939	Truck crash, Castill de Peones, Burgos
Hardt, Jurgen	2/Lt	07-04-1939	Truck crash, Castill de Peones, Burgos
Hinners, Heinrich	W/O	10-01-1938	Nephritic infection, Burgos
Mittelstorb, Heinrich	2/Lt	07-04-1939	Truck crash, Castill de Peones, Burgos
Ohlhorst, Heinz	1/Lt	15-05-1937	Duodenum spasm, Salamanca
Schaumburg, Walter	W/O	24-07-1937	Hand grenade, San Roque, Cadiz
Spranger, Rudolf	2/Lt	07-04-1939	Truck crash, Castill de Peones, Burgos
Wolf*, Ricardo	1/Lt	01-08-1937	Died of typhus, Burgos

12

"Negrillos" at the Academia de Guerra Química

After a personal talk with Generalissimo Franco, on 10 January 1937 Artillery *corone* Juan Izquierdo Croselles, who had published a book entitled "*Manual de Guerra Química*" as early as 1931, as a result of the knowledge obtained while he was posted at the *Fábric* Nacional de Productos Químicos at La Marañosa, took charge of the *Servicio de Guerre Química* (Chemical Warfare Service) and started an urgent reorganization. On the 22ⁿᵈ o. the same month, the composition of the *Junta Técnica Nacional de Defensa Química* wa: approved.

The spark of these decisions was the use of tea gas bombs (chloroacetophenon, or CN gas) agains the Alcázar in Toledo on 8 October 1936, followed by other bombings with smoke and incendiary bombs on the 9ᵗʰ and 15ᵗʰ of that same month. There are also othe unconfirmed references to actions carried out by the self-called "Red Militia," such as the gas attack on the airfield and the railway station at Talavera de la Reina in September 1936, and the use of tear gases in the Sierra de Guadarrama, not to forget the production of chlorine in Valencia. It should also be reminded that in the minds

Individual protection equipment from Germany: suit, N-24 mask type and Draegger detector. Germany and Italy supplied large amounts of equipment of this sort. (Authors)

f all the officers who had fought the war in Africa there was the reminiscence of the use f gases against the Rif fighters, generalized after the Annual Disaster[23] and the subsequent 1ass murder of Spanish prisoners, apart from its production in Melilla and at La Marañosa, nd the fresh memories of its massive use in the Great War, despite the 1899 and 1907 The Iague Treaties.

In October 1936, with these precedents, the vice-chancellor of Saragossa University, Ir. Calamita, and *teniente coronel* de Diego had started studies for the production of hoking and tear gases and a field detector in the territory of the *5ª División*. The Sociedad Anónima Energía e Industrias Aragonesas (E.I.A.) factory, at Sabiñánigo, Huesca, was hosen and, by early 1937, the installation of a phosgene workshop started. But in the ollowing month, the enemy artillery bombed the factory and other nearby objectives and, hould the phosgene be the cause of all that shelling, it was decided to move production to he rearguard.

For all this, the Battle of the Jarama River (February 1937), which started with the apture of the Pindoque bridge, near La Marañosa, gave the impression that the Nationalist ommand was seeking to outflank Madrid from the south, precisely in the direction which llowed it very soon to occupy the Fábrica de Gases,[24] which was found stripped down. 'reviously, on 19 July, a large part of its officers had been shot in the vicinity.

Decontamination practice. In the foreground is a gas victim. (Gas unit. Ávila, 1937). (via Carlos Murias)

Those in charge of the factory had placed some chlorine bottles in the valley floor near La Marañosa in order to hold back the Nationalist advance, but the hasty red retreat through that same valley might have caused a disaster in their own ranks.

A report by the gas specialist of the *Legión Cóndor* (named Manne) addressed to the German Military Attaché in the Nationalist area, *Oberstlt* von Funck, says: "...it can be stated that the Reds have made poison gases (mustard) at La Marañosa (occupied on February 1937). Written information says that the workers filled bombs and grenades with gas (...). It is the opinion of *capitán* Blanco (who was to be the next Production Manager in the factory) that all the equipment dismantled from La Marañosa has been moved to Alcoy where there is a chlorine factory..." Manne confirms that the chlorine tanks intended to stop the attack on La Marañosa numbered about fifty. In April 1937, with elements from the different divisions and columns, the *Servicio de Guerra Química* (S.G.Q.) was established in Salamanca. The Nationalist Army organized a school team attached to the Generalissimo's HQs in Salamanca, and an Intervention Unit with personnel from the different units then in Valladolid, which later moved to Ávila. Their badge was a yellow rhombus with arms or a black St Andrew's cross in the middle. The decontamination practice carried out by the school team at the time consisted of a cleansing of small areas previously sprayed with sneezing agents, tear and mustard gas, and lewisite.

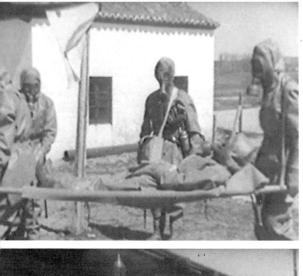

Personnel evacuation and decontamination exercises at the *Escuela de Guerra Química*, Salamanca, 1937. Decontamination practice, Ávila, November 1937. (both Authors)

Hardly a month afterwards, the attacks took place near the village of Cilleruelo de Bricia, on the Santander front, on 30 June, 4, 4, 6, 23, and 24 July 1937. In total, nearly 200 artillery shells from the First World War, with tear, sneezing agents, mustard, chlorine, and phosgene were fired. *Teniente coronel* Sagardía himself, who was in command of the column, the size of about a brigade, was wounded.

Information from the SIFNE (*Servicio de Información de la Fontera Nordeste de España*)[25] dated early July 1937 in Toulouse made the following warning, "...they intend to make a sham attack with harmless gases as a deception on the Nationalist High Command, to force it to use poison gases and then launch a big press campaign in all the countries sympathizing with the Red government, even with the dispatch of International Commissions, which will certainly confirm that there were no gas victims in the Nationalist ranks, but indeed on the Red side." From this report, it was clear for the Nationalist *Servicio de Información Militar* (SIM) that the aggression was premeditated. For a long time, the SIM had been gathering news that the enemy was seeking an escalade to cause an international reaction in their favor, which would also make them free to use gases, thus preventing the fall of Bilbao.

It was in this context that the proposal from the chief general of *Movilización, Instrucción y Recuperación* (*M.I.R*), dated 9 June 1937, was born. It was addressed to the Generalissimo's HQs to train temporary 2nd lieutenants of the Chemical Warfare Service "...for the duration of the campaign..." with mobilized soldiers picked among civil engineers or chemistry or pharmacy graduates, through courses announced in a restricted way and not published in the *Boletín Oficial del Estado*. The proposal was quickly accepted on 8 July by means of a confirmatory order signed by the chief general of the General Staff, and the abovementioned school team became the Chemical Warfare Academy in Salamanca.

Previously, from 2 to 9 May 1937, a course had been given with German instructors at the Fábrica de Armas de Toledo—at that time the HQs of the Chemical Warfare Service—with a view to the establishment of a defensive gas battalion.

Coronel Izquierdo Croselles, medical *teniente coronel* Usera Rodríguez, Artillery *comandantes* Martínez Ortiz and Crespo Granja, *captains* of the same corps Serrano Navas and de Blas Álvarez (the latter was a chemist and pharmacist and author of the book "*Química de Guerra*," first published in 1934), and Artillery honorary *alférez* de Izquierdo Aguilar took part in this course. The so-called "*Grupo negrillo*" also took part, and was

Decontamination practice, Avila, November 1937. (via Carlos Murias)

Nationalist decontamination unit with hypoclorite backpack equipment. The suits and N-24 masks are German. (via Carlos Murias)

Nationalist decontamination unit with hypoclorite dispensers (originally used for fertilizing). The tractor is a Fordson, used by the Artillery in the 1920s. (via Carlos Murias)

later attached to the Salamanca Academy, initially made up of the following German commanders:

Capt Alfred Manne	Teacher and main instructor
Lt Alfons Huebner	Auxiliary teacher and instructor
Lt Julius Junghans	Idem
1/Lt Johann Millen	Idem
1/Lt Karl Mueller	Idem

All of them had arrived in Spain in January 1937. The captain and the 1st lieutenants remained at the Salamanca Academy until May 1939, whereas the 2nd lieutenants left the country in July 1937, relieved on 1 January 1938 by the following officers:

Lt Karl E. Reckel	(returned to Germany 01-03-38)
1/Lt Walter Heitmann	(returned to Germany 01-07-38)
NCO Alfred Stammwitz	(returned to Germany 01-12-38)

The nature of the service made it advisable to give a restricted character to the organization of the courses, for which reason neither the notices nor the appointments were ever published in the *Boletín Oficial del Estado*, with the only exception being the first course (although without specifying which arm or corps the temporary 2nd lieutenants belonged to). All the documents regarding the courses were restricted and were processed by means of verbal orders, the revelation of the notices being carried out through discrete advertising among the soldiers that met the specifications.

The officer courses were given in Salamanca with an average length of twenty-five days, completing the training of about two hundred 1st lieutenants and temporary 2nd lieutenants, apart from other officers, NCOs, and civilians.

Namely, the courses were the following, in chronological order:

COURSES GIVEN AT THE *ESCUELA DE GUERRA QUÍMICA*

Nº	Ranks	Length	Students	Graduates
1	1/Lts - Acting 2/Lts	25-07 / 18-08-37	38	36
2	1/Lts - Acting 2/Lts	25-08 / 18-09-37	52	48
3	1/Lts - Acting 2/Lts	05-10 / 30-10-37	40	39
s/n	"K"* Officers	05-09 / 13-09-37	70 approx.	-
4	Acting Officers	28-11 / 23-12-37	30	20
5	Acting Officers	01-04 / 24-05-38	35	34
4	Military Veterinaries	14-07 / 24-07-38	-	-
4	Acting Sgts.	19-09 / 14-10-38	-	-
s/n	J.E.P.C.**	17-10 / 26-10-38	20	-
s/n	Military Doctors	05-11 / 15-11-38	17	-
2	Acting Sgts.	19-11 / 15-12-38	-	-
2	Military Veterinaries	24-11 / 03-12-38	-	-
s/n	M.D.P.P.C.***	12-12 / 20-12-38	20	-
6	Acting Officers ****	15-12-38/24-01-39	(called off)	

Both sergeant courses were given to the corporals and soldiers posted at the Chemical Warfare Service.

* "K" Officers of the Spanish-Italian Mixed Brigades (*Tropas Legionarias*)

** *Jefes de Equipo de Desimpregnación de Población Civil* (Civil Population Decontamination Team Chiefs)

*** *Médicos de Defensa Pasiva de Población Civil* (Civil Population Passive Defense Doctors)

**** 99 places

An analysis of the development of these sixteen courses reveals a first phase of huge organizational work and urgent officer training in order to supply the fledgling "light" (one per division) and "heavy" (one per Army Corps or Group of Divisions) teams with officers and NCOs; this phase extends to the second half of 1937. Then there is a sudden stoppage of four months and, later, the training of *Sanidad Militar* officers and *Cuadros de Defensa Pasiva* (Civil Defense) started, in a phase that seems to seek a "deepening" of the organization of the Nationalist *Defensa Antigás*, including the training of NCOs. Finally, the enormous effort carried out at the academy by late 1938 must be stressed, with four simultaneous courses in November and December, certainly as a result of the persistent news from the Nationalist intelligence services regarding the foreseeable use of gases by the Red Army (it should be reminded that there was communist influence on the so-called Republican Army, where only after Casado's uprising, in March 1939, were the revolutionary symbols and contents suppressed) in order to prevent the fall of Catalonia. The rapid collapse of the resistance with the capture of Tarragona on 15 January 1939 and the arrival in the French border on 10 February, rendered the last course for temporary officers unnecessary.

13

German Advisers for the *Escuela Naval*

In the last months of 1937, the then *Comandante General* of the Maritime Department of Cadiz, *almirante*[26] Francisco Bastarreche, called a series of meetings with chief officers of the Nationalist and German navies to discuss the usefulness of the participation of German instructors in the training of the students and ratings of the *Escuela Naval Militar*, at San Fernando, Cadiz. Apart from the admiral, on the Spanish side the meetings were attended by *capitán de fragata*[27] Manuel Ferrer Antón, Director of the *Escuela*; *capitán de corbeta*[28] Ricardo Calvar González-Aller, Deputy Director; and the Navy Service Corps *comandante* Antonio Escolano Moreno, third Commander of the school.

W/O Alfred Doerschmann, one of the German instructors from the *Drohne*, at work at the *Escuela Naval*. (via César O'Donnell)

On the German side were *Fregattenkapitän* Meyer-Döhner, Naval Attaché, head of the German Naval mission, and *Korvettenkapitän* Lange, a member of the mission.

It was concluded at the meetings that it was necessary to count on *"negrillo"* instructors to help the Spanish teaching personnel in their training task of the discipline and the military spirit of the prospective members of the *Marina*.[29]

On 23 December 1937, *almirante* Bastarreche sent a letter to *general* Orgaz so that the latter, as previously discussed, would send a team of German instructors to the *Escuela Naval Militar* at San Fernando. Given the diversity of personnel to be trained (midshipmen, candidates, students of the Service Corps and ratings), the admiral pointed out the convenience of sending a *"negrillo"* chief officer previously so that he, "...on the spot, and with a knowledge of our needs, would determine which and how many (instructors) should come...." The course, according to the admiral, was scheduled to start on 10 January.

The *Jefatura de M.I.R.* sent an official letter to Colonel von Thoma explaining the request of the *Comandante General* of the Maritime Department of Cadiz for the dispatch of instructors. The

Spanish-German 1/Lt instructor Joachim Canaris. He was a resident in Spain (via César O'Donnell)

1/Lt instructor Erich Schoenfeld, from the Kuestrin Infantry Regiment, teaching "closed order" at the *Escuela Naval* ratings. (via César O'Donnell)

German was told that the instructors would basically take care of "...the tactical training from a purely formal view with some housekeeping rules for the students...," and that it was convenient to send, sooner rather than later, as the course would start on 10 January, a chief officer or an officer "...so that he could specify the needs on the spot and determine the composition of the team, which might be naval."

And so it was on 11 January, that Orgaz informed Bastarreche that the team was already established and ready for impending induction.

That "*negrillo*" team was made up of the following members:

- Team Chief: Col Erich Grosse (from the Infantry Regiment in Ludwisburg). Arrived in Spain as a Militia instructor in February 1937. In May, became Chief Instructor at the Toledo Infantry Academy.
- Instructors:
- 1/Lt Frederick von Schweinitz, who joined the "*negrillo*" instructor teams in September 1937 from the Berlin Infantry Regiment. (On 1 May 1938 he was relieved by 1/Lt Wilhelm Hantelmann who, in turn, was relieved by 1/Lt Bernard Kammann on 17 May). He served as a Company CO.
- 1/Lt Erich Rose. Arrived in Spain in June 1937 from the Ludwisburg Infantry Regiment. Joined the *Legión* in August 1938, where he remained for the rest of the war.
- 1/Lt Joachim Canaris, resident in Spain. From January to April 1937, trained militia officers, then posted to different academies from May that same year on.

1/Lt Boche, from *Gruppe Drohne*, training the brigade of prospective Navy Service Corps Temporary Second Lieutenants. (via César O'Donnell)

- 2/Lt Johann Hoffmann, resident in Spain. Joined as academy instructor in November 1937. Promoted to 1st lieutenant on 20 March 1938 when serving at the *Escuela Naval*.
- 2/Lt Gerhard Boche, from the Neuruppin Tank Regiment, arrived in Spain in October 1936 as a tank instructor. In May 1937 joined the Infantry instructor teams organized in *Gruppe Imker*.
- 2/Lt Erich Schoenfeld, from the Kuestrin Infantry Regiment, arrived in Spain in November 1937 and stayed until December the following year.
- NCO Alfred Doerschmann. Arrived in Spain from the Bamberg Tank Regiment in October 1936 and posted to the tank Workshop. On 1 May 1937 posted to several academics as an Infantry instructor.
- NCO Helmuth Goennawein. Arrived in Spain from the Döberitz Infantry Regiment in June 1937, as an Infantry instructor.

Three views of the head of the *"negrillo"* instructor team at the *Escuela Naval* at San Fernando, *Oberstleutnant* Erich Grosse. This German field officer, who was previously head instructor at the Toledo Infantry Academy, arrived in Spain in May 1937. (top and center: Authors; bottom: César O'Donnell)

The course started on schedule, on 10 January 1938. The German team made its presentation on Monday, 17 January, with a ceremony that took place at the *Panteón de Marinos Ilustres*,[30] in the presence of a formation of teachers and students. They stayed at the Hotel Atlántico in Cadiz, then requisitioned by the *Armada*.[31] The Germans organized themselves in three groups of three instructors on permanent duty 24 hours a day at the *Escuela*, every three days.

The course length was nineteen weeks, to train the *Escuela Naval Militar* students, as well as, for shorter periods, the prospective temporary 2nd lieutenants of the *Armada* Service Corps, the *Escuela Naval* ratings, and the Cádiz *Comandancia General del Departamento* ratings, as well as the *Infantería de Marina* musicians, with German march scores being supplied by the battleship *Deutschland* for the latter.

The main objectives of the training carried out by the Germans were discipline, physical education, hygiene and policy, and closed order training with parade step (particularly the 114-step German one).

W/O instructor Helmuth Goennawein, from the Döberitz Regiment. (via César O'Donnell)

1/Lt instructor Erich Rose, from the Ludwigsberg Infantry Regiment. In 1938 he joined the Spanish *Legión* for the duration. (via César O'Donnell)

Every Sunday there was a mass at the *Escuela* chapel that was attended to by the Germans who were on duty that day.

On 14 April the student contingent increased, after the Marine temporary 2nd lieutenants had joined the *Escuela*. For that reason, it was necessary to augment proportionally the presence of German instructors. 1/Lt Erich Rose, who was appointed director of the two-month course, had the following auxiliary instructor personnel, supplied by several Infantry academies operating in the Nationalist area:

- 1/Lt Johannes Gebhardt. Arrived in Spain in November 1937, then joined the Infantry Academy at Jerez de la Frontera as Section CO.
- NCO Helmuth Sasche. Arrived in Spain in October 1936 as a tank instructor, and in May 1937 became Infantry instructor at the San Roque Academy, and thence to the *Escuela Naval*.
- NCO Ludwig Menke. Arrived in Spain in December 1937 and joined the Granada Infantry Academy as Section CO. Returned to Germany in March 1939.

By 1 March 1938, the *negrillo* group at the *Escuela Naval* had already trained eighty students and one hundred and sixty ratings, a figure that was to increase, for these instructors stayed until the end of the war.

1/Lt instructor Johan Hoffmann. He was living in Spain and joined in as Infantry academies instructor in November 1937, (via César O'Donnell)

1/Lt instructor Gerhard Boche, *Gruppe Drohne*. (via César O'Donnell)

14

Gruppe Lucht, von Thoma's Artillery

The Origins of German Artillery Training in Spain

On 7 October 1937, a notice was published in the *Boletín Oficial del Estado* for a course for Artillery reserve 2nd lieutenants and 1st lieutenants, for theoretical and practical training to substantiate their aptitude for the rank above. It was the first time this was heard of in the Nationalist area, and it was the Artillery Academy in Segovia—commanded by *coronel* Félix Beltrán de Lis Balderrábano—which had the chance to establish the syllabi for the course.

The course started in Segovia on 3 November, and was attended by sixty-eight reserve 2nd lieutenants and eighty-four 1st lieutenants. The end of the classes and of the training of the reserve 2nd lieutenants, qualified to hold the rank above (the course lasted a month), was on the saint patron of the corps, Saint Barbara, on 4 December. Because of its own

(Authors)

haracteristics, the aptitude course for captains had more exhaustive syllabi, which entitled andidates to command a battery in campaign, and thus the length was three months.

On 6 January 1938 the course was interrupted for a while because of the need for the tudents of this academy to go on general exercises to be carried out in Ávila and Cabezón de Pisuerga, Valladolid, directed by German and Italian officers respectively. A tremendous nowstorm forced the cancellation of those in Ávila and saw those at Cabezón reduced to a minimum, the latter being attended by the head of the *legionario* instructors, *colonnello* Rivolta.

It was already at the preparation of these exercises to be carried out in Ávila that the ack of artillery equipment, not available to the Germans for training in Spain, became obvious. The cancellation of the exercises was not an obstacle, though, to Colonel von

German W/O instructor of *Grupo de Instrucción de Artillería*. The training on the assembly and cleaning of the Mauser rifle was one of the German tasks. (M. Álvaro, via Raúl Arias)

Thoma, head of the whole contingent of the *"negrillo"* instructors. Aware of that lack, h
announced to *general* Orgaz that, thanks to the steps he had taken, assorted armament an
artillery equipment was to be sent from Germany. This included some more equipment fo
the Infantry and Engineers, which had already been asked for by the *Jefatura* and offere
by the Germans on several occasions, so no further steps were required from the *Jefatur*
de M.I.R.

The weapons that the German High Command decided to send to Spain to put an en
to the lack of artillery training equipment were two of the most modern howitzers availabl
from the 3rd Reich at the moment, the 15-cm *schwere Feld Haubitze* sFH and the 10.5-cm
leichte Feld Haubitze leFH.

Equipment Arrives
Once the equipment for the three corps became available, the *Jefatura* studied th
establishment of several fully-Spanish units "...that will interpret our tactical doctrine an
will allow, once these units are operational, to continue those information courses directed.
explained, and carried out by fully-Spanish means. And it all is in response to the training
mission entrusted to this *Jefatura*...."

Thus an Artillery Group, an Infantry Battalion, and a Mixed Sapper-Miner/Signals
Company were established at the same time at Monasterio de Rodilla (Burgos), Toledo.
and Burgos respectively.

By early January 1938, *general* Orgaz sent an official letter to the Chief General o
the *6ª División* reporting that in a short time a two-battery group to be used on training and
popularization tasks was to be established in the province of Burgos. Those batteries were

10.5-cm LeFH 18 howitzer at Monasterio de Rodilla, Burgos. (Authors)

Two scenes showing different training aspects on the light 105/26 howitzers. Copies were made in Spain from 1943 on, in several versions. (both Authors)

administratively attached to *11 Regimiento Ligero de Artillería*, and their assigned numbers were 53ª for the light one and 54ª for the heavy one. *Capitán* Antonio Lucena, then posted at the *Jefatura de M.I.R,* was entrusted the command of the Artillery Training Group—for this is how the unit was called.

Capitán Antonio Lucena Gómez was a career officer of the Artillery Corps, at whose Academy he had graduated as a 1st lieutenant in 1922 with the 210th Course. Promoted to captain in 1928, his last posting before the war broke out was the *Grupo Mixto nº 3* in Las Palmas, Canary Islands. By early 1937 he was posted to the *Jefatura de M.I.R.,* under *general* Orgaz's orders.

The German howitzers

The light howitzer battery was made up of four 10.5-cm leFH 18 (*leichte Feld Haubitzer* 18) guns. These howitzers were made by Rheinmetall in the late twenties, entered service in the German Army in 1935, and eventually became the core of the German light field howitzers during the Second World War. With a twin-spare carriage, this gun was well designed and had a maximum range of 10,800 m and a total weight of 1,900 kg.

The heavy howitzers were the 15-cm sFH 18 (*schwere Feld Haubitzer* 18, actually the caliber was 149/29.5) model. And, although also designed by Rheinmetall in the same period as the former, the carriage was by Krupp, and was used both for this and the 105/52 K 18 (*Kanone* 18) gun, also used in Spain. It entered service in Germany in 1933 and saw remarkable success during the Second World War, also used by the Italian and Finnish armies. With a maximum range of 13,800 m and a weight of 5,342 kg, it was an atypical

howitzer due to the long length barrel (4.44 m), which advised for a separate tactical transport: the barrel or the one hand and the carriage on the other.

On 9 March, *capitán* Lucena asked *general* Orgaz to issue suitable orders to supply the group with full clothing for the two hundred and fifteen men. One month later, on 6 April, recently promoted *comandante* Antonio Lucena signed the composition of the group and, a week a later, the *Comandante General de Artillería*, García Pallasar, reported that it had been assigned six tractors "...from those that have to come to Badajoz...." These were American Caterpillars, about two hundred and fifty of which were used by the Nationalist side during the conflict.

Comandante Lucena also asked for ammunition for the guns of both batteries, for he was aware that the Germans had supplied just 1,200 shells per battery; a very small figure, but absolutely necessary to start training.

The Group is Ready

On 2 May 1938, restricted official letter n° 5661/35.582 of the *2ª Sección de la Jefatura de M.I.R.* reported to the Generalissimo that the *Grupo de Instrucción de Artillería* was ready for front service but for the delivery of transport equipment and ammunition, which, according to Colonel von Thoma's calculations, involved 4,000 shells per battery per month. Two weeks later, the C.G.G. said that it was not convenient to take the Group to the front, for the acquisition of additional shells required hard currency.

Four views of the transport and emplacement of the heavy 150-mm howitzer battery. On training duties, a pair of oxen was used to tow it (see top picture). (all Authors)

Von Thoma's official letter had left it clear that property of the Group equipment remained German, and that it had been made available to the Nationalist Army just for training. For that reason, if the Nationalist authorities wanted to make use of the guns on military operations, permission should be granted from the German High Command. In any case, von Thoma assured "...because of their performance, they can be efficiently used in all sorts of tactical circumstances, even under the most difficult ones...."

It is very important to stress that *general* García Pallasar's answer to the *M.I.R* official letter was forceful, "...it is considered to be in the powers of the High Command whether to seek or not permission from Germany to use the batteries in question in our Army operations, but should it be seen necessary, it has to be done on condition that they must be subordinated to Spanish command, with no limitation whatsoever nor difference in use as compared to the other Army batteries."

The German instructors

The artillery equipment, apart from the corresponding spares, came with a group of German instructors, entrusted with the mission of training the Spanish personnel in its use. It was headed by *Oberstleutnant* Walter Lucht, as Artillery Chief Instructor of the *"negrillo"* team, under von Thoma's direct orders.

The team was made up of Majors Lehmann and Kaul, 1/Lts Rohbach (armorer) and Tiche, and 2/Lts Petzold, Bodlée, Rauchfuss, Heidecke, Skorzewesky, and von Gross, as well as W/Os Hillmann and Manningel. (**Note:** all these officers and NCOs are mentioned

Signals were a very important aspect of the *Grupo de Instrucción de Artillería*. The corps was supplied with modern powerful German radios, operated by the Spanish soldiers after training from the German instructors. (Authors)

The full 105/26 howitzer battery. (C. Díez via Raúl Arias)

in the documents researched for this work, although the general listings of *Gruppe Thoma - Academias* only include Lucht, Kaul, Tiehe, and Petzold)

On 19 August, *comandante* Lucena sent *general* Orgaz the schedule of the group's Training Plan, established by Colonel Lucht, to be submitted to the *M.I.R.* HQs office. The schedule detailed the training activities of the German personnel, as well as its distribution for the training of the Spanish officers, NCOs, and troops. A week later, on 26 August, it was Colonel Lucht himself who sent the *M.I.R.* HQs office the schedule, after enlarging the one submitted the week before by *comandante* Lucena.

Certainly, the goodwill and the work carried out by the Germans for the drawing up of the exhaustive training plan were of no use for, on the following day (the 28th), Generalissimo Franco issued orders to the effect that both batteries of the Artillery Training Group, so far at Monasterio de Rodilla, be put at the disposal of the *Ejército del Norte* for the duration of the operations in the Ebro area.

A new battery

Shortly before the start of the operations in the Ebro area—although the precise arrival date is unknown—a third German battery armed with Rheinmetall 10.5-cm K 18 guns, on Krupp carriages (105/52), which arrived in Spain like the others through the *Legión Cóndor*, joined the Training Group. It was assigned at once administratively—like the

An impressive three-quarter view of the German 105/52 K 18 gun. (Authors)

howitzers—to *Regimiento de Artillería Ligero n° 11*, based in Burgos, in whose organic structure it was integrated, to become *n° 58* in the numbering of the batteries established by this unit during the war. It was immediately sent to the Ebro area, taking part with the other two howitzer batteries in the Nationalist counteroffensive on the Sierra de Caballs sector, in the Corbera area, firing on several land objectives, including several bridges over the river and a railway line.

On 14 November, the head of the group got orders from the C.G.G. to leave the area for Híjar, which were carried out at once. After a week at Híjar, Colonel Lucht ordered *comandante* Lucena to get back to Burgos with the group, to restart the training mission for which it had been established. But because of the lack of a suitable place to park the equipment, both in Burgos and at its former location at Monasterio de Rodilla—where mortar units were based on the organization and training phase—the *M.I.R* command decided to make them to stay at Briviesca, Burgos, the order being forwarded to Colonels von Thoma and Lucht.

Rheinmetall 10.5-cm K 18 gun on Krupp carriage. The *Grupo de Instrucción de Artillería* got a battery in the summer of 1938, which joined the two howitzer batteries already in Spain. (Authors)

Training and New batteries for the Nationalist Army

On 17 December 1938, Colonel Lucht visited the then interim head of *Movilización, Instrucción y Recuperación, coronel* Fernández Tamarit, to whom he explained that twenty-five field batteries would soon arrive for the Nationalist Army from Germany. Two of them should be settled at Briviesca with German instructors for perfecting courses for the prospective Spanish teachers who, in turn, should train Nationalist training teams in their original Armies.

For that reason, Lucht asked permission to give 21-day training courses at Briviesca that should be attended—in the German's opinion—by two 1st lieutenants, two 2nd lieutenants, twenty-five sergeants, twenty-five corporals, and fifty soldiers. Tamarit took into consideration these and other proposals by Lucht and sent them to the C.G.G. Staff where—to say it plainly—they were rejected, "...the military operations do not allow to organize the courses as envisaged by that Colonel (Lucht) neither with the frequency stated, nor with the personnel requested, belonging to a same Army...."

At long last, after an exchange of notes, the C.G.G. allowed a 7.7-cm gun course, to be attended by four officers, a warrant officer, fourteen sergeants, thirty-five corporals, and fifty second class artillerists, all of them from *10º Regimiento Ligero*. This course was given at Briviesca and was to be the first and last, mostly because the end of the conflict was approaching.

The two howitzer batteries of the Training Group, the two 7.7-cm gun batteries and the 105/52-mm battery obtained by the *M.I.R* HQs office were left in Spain at the disposal of the Army, and the bill was included in the General Accounts of the *Legión Cóndor*, submitted by Germany in May that same year.

From January to March 1938, the *Escuela de Artillería* at Monasterio de Rodilla trained fourteen officers, sixty-three sergeants, and three hundred and eighty soldiers in the use of the 10.5 and 15-cm howitzer batteries. Besides, *Gruppe Thoma* trained thirty Spanish officers, eighty sergeants, and five hundred soldiers until March 1938 in the use of the 7.7-cm FK 16 field guns sent by Germany by early 1937.

(Authors)

TRAINING AND USE OF GERMAN ARTILLERY

"...We arrived in Spain in January and the Artillery Group was distributed for training. For us, there was no nicer task than training the Spanish soldiers in the use of German equipment and in accordance with German procedures. After the training was ended with a live fire exercise, we only had a longing, to go to the front and prove that the training had bore fruit. Our desires would be accomplished.

Personnel and equipment were sent to the vanguard by rail, whereas the Germans would be driven by Kübelwagen. First we enjoyed the views, it was hard to believe we were at war. Later, on the contrary, the image changed; there the war machinery had done its work. Our commander went on ahead with the battery commanders to find the settlement area, where we arrived by dusk.

Then the preparation of the settlements began and we witnessed the soldiers to carry out their tasks quickly and precisely. The difficulties were those inherent to the ground and thus, the mountains, stones, and the narrow roads that we travelled across were no simple obstacles for the heavy batteries. But the encouraging words made the Spanish soldiers overcome them. Officers and calculators were busy all night long so that the attack could start the following morning.

The trial shots were fired between 07,45 and 08,00 hrs and were only enough to prove again that the preparation by our people had been exemplary and precise. They started fire so quickly that they achieved the same goals as other batteries with more ammunition. Once all the batteries stopped firing, there was total calm (...)

At 10,00 hrs all the batteries should start firing, the watch hands walked too slowly and every ten minutes we looked at the time. In the meantime, the COs of the Infantry companies approached us and used our sights to find a path for the assault. At 10 sharp, over 200 guns started firing. (...) Our fire rate was good, and one after another, the bunkers were destroyed by our 15-cm shells. Stones and sandbags flew into the air and big rock masses rolled downhill. (...)

At 10,30 hrs the bugle call of the *1ª División de Navarra* could be heard and, resolutely, the courageous soldiers hurried to the enemy positions. While our Infantry was in its trenches, they got grazing fire from enemy machine guns placed on a flank. But the Artillery was there to protect them, wiping out the machine gun nests with our fire.

Our Artillery Group had proved it knew how to do its work, and would also do it again two days later. The target was a concrete bridge over the Ebro, the only one the enemy had got for supplies. As this could not be hit using ground observers, air observation was required. With 84 shells we scored two direct hits, so the bridge was rendered useless for vehicle traffic. How much the enemy was dependent on that bridge was to be revealed the following day, when the enemy aircraft looked for us until, at night, we began to attract intense fire. They had found us in the dark and made harassing fire, so the following day we changed settlements.

In the meantime, the enemy was building an improvised bridge. These can always be destroyed and it should be noticed that, with 70 shells, we managed to get rid of three such bridges. Thanks to that, it would not be possible any more for the enemy to move their batteries nor other equipment to a safe area beyond the river. Everything would fall in our hands.

Our work was a total success...."

Excerpted from the book "*Deutsche kampfen in Spanien.*"

15

Other German Training Groups

The 7.7-cm minethrower advisers

In January 1937, eighty 7.58-cm mine throwers arrived in Seville from Germany and were distributed to the arm depots of the *Ejército del Norte* and the *Ejército del Sur*, without previous training for the personnel.

The Ehrhardt mine throwers were phased-in in Germany around 1911, although in 1916 they were highly modified and their aspect changed to their definitive configuration. During the First World War their use became extraordinarily widespread, and the German Army had over 13,000 units at the end of the conflict. Its 1,325-meter range, and ambivalent use as close support guns or as trench mortar, had this gun classified as a field mortar and, as a result, it was earmarked as a suitable weapon for Infantry use.

Several Spanish soldiers training in the use of the Erdhardt 7.58-cm minelaunchers surveyed by the "negrillo" instructors of *Gruppe Issendorff*. Granada Academia. (Authors)

Once the equipment was distributed, sixty mine throwers were assigned to the *Ejército del Norte* and another twenty to the *Ejército del Sur*, and the high command proceeded with the organization of the units entrusted with its use and the training of the personnel assigned.

The *Ejército del Norte* followed a vague criterion in its distribution and organization, alternatively assigning its use to Infantry and Artillery units. Thus, the *6° Cuerpo de Ejército* entrusted the organization of the mine thrower units to the Artillery Corps, and so a battery was established (the *9ª Batería* of *Regimiento 11° Lige*) with three sections and a total of nine guns. The *Brigada de Navarra*, of the same *Cuerpo de Ejército* (Army Corps) grouped them in a battery attached to the *2° Regimiento de Montaña*, with seven guns commanded by a captain. In the *8° Cuerpo de Ejército* a mine thrower unit was established, divided into six sections attached to the forces operating in Asturias, designated as the *14ª Batería* of the *11° Regimiento Ligero*, with twenty-four mine throwers. The *Parque de Artillería*[32] in Burgos supplied two guns to the *1ª Bandera Irlandesa*[33] (at Talavera), another two to the *10ª Bandera de La Legión*, and four to the *Regimiento Ligero n° 11*. The *Parque de Artillería* in Valladolid supplied two guns to the *Bandera Irlandesa* and one each to several battalions.

However, the *Ejército del Sur* unified its criterion regarding the corps that should use them, and entrusted them only to the Infantry, with four-gun sections established in the "*Cádiz*," "*Pavia*," "*Lepanto*," "*Castilla*," and "*Sevilla*" regiments.

Wilhelm von Thoma established a school with his men to train the prospective gun-crew members for the mine throwers, and entrusted it to *Oblt* Werner Haag, with *Lt* Paul Eilenberger, who arrived in Spain in January 1937, as second in command. The latter remained in his posting until the end of the war.

From January 1937 to March 1938, the *Gruppe Thoma* trained a total of one hundred and seventy-seven officers, two hundred and twenty sergeants, and about 2,000 soldiers in the use of the 7.58-cm mine throwers.

MINE THROWER INSTRUCTORS

NAME	RANK	PERIOD	REMARKS
Eilenberger, Paul	1/Lt	01-37/ 05-39	Mine thrower School Instructor
Haag, Werner	Capt	01-37/ 05 39	Mine thrower School Chief Instructor
Heipp,	2/Lt	01-37/ 01-38	Mine thrower School Instructor

(Authors)

The *Academia de Automovilismo* in Corunna

The *Jefatura de M.I.R.* asked Colonel von Thoma, Tank Inspector in Nationalist Spain and Academy Chief Instructor (*Imker Ausbilder*), for the presence of *negrillo* officers in the training of the temporary automobile NCOs, the course that was to take place in Corunna from late September 1937.

Colonel von Thoma sent an official letter to *general* Orgaz on 10 September to confirm the presence of German instructors in those courses. In accordance with the indications from the German, the School Director included in the course syllabus "strict formal military training for the soldiers, to show military behavior, knowledge and use of arms (pistol and rifle), concise knowledge of behavior in combat, vehicle camouflage and choice of suitable places...."

On 11 September the following *negrillo* instructors, all of them from the Infantry academies operating in Spain, were posted to the Corunna Academy:

Martenstein, August	Col
Mueller, Adolf	1/Lt
Lamprecht, Adolf	2/Lt
Schlatterer, Alfred	2/Lt
Schuetze, Heinrich	2/Lt

The speed in the posting of these personnel was really impressive. *General* Orgaz sent the *Coronel Inspector de Automovilismo*—the authority on whom depended the notices for the automobile course—an official letter reporting the posting of the five *negrillo* instructors, with a letter from von Thoma enclosed, along with some of the instructions in force at the Military Academies regarding the collaboration of these instructors and a confidential letter on the same subject.

(Canario Azaola)

The instructions essentially referred to the relationships between the Spanish personnel of the academies and the German instructors:

"The relationships of the Academy directorate with the group of *negrillo* instructors who are coming to complement the teacher staff, given the circumstance that there are no active officers physically fit to carry out the tactical and practice fire classes, shall be regulated by the general rules of military discipline. The Colonel Director acts as head with full powers and responsibility, and the Head of the instructors team shall be subordinated to him, with whom he shall keep direct contact regarding everything related to the team and through whom he shall issue orders and instructions he might find suitable to the rest of the officers that make it up and whatever inquiries the latter might have for the Colonel Director. The Head of the team, within the general rules to be established by the Director, shall enjoy independence for the distribution of work and allocation of missions to the team officers. The Colonel shall see to whatever proposals the Head of the team might have for him that are within the possibilities of the latter and might contribute to the better running of the training. As regards the Head of the team, he shall try to carry out his mission bearing in mind that he must combine it with the rest of the classes and the other aspects of the officer training (sic). As regards the awards and punishments that it should be necessary to administer, this shall always be done so after a well-reasoned proposal explained to the Director of Studies or the Academy Director. The spiritual mutual understanding resulting from the similarity of ideas and feelings must be translated at the Academy into a cordial and affectionate relationship between the *negrillo* officer corps and the Spanish counterpart. The former

Enlistment oath of Temporary Second Lieutenants at the Main Square of Salamanca. The students kneel at consecration. (Authors)

greatly honour us by their understanding of our fate; in this enterprise of universal magnitude in the service of true civilization, Spain is not sparing sacrifices and feels the encouragement of her comrades, the '*negrillos*' to whom everlasting gratitude is to be paid...."

Regarding *general* Orgaz's confidential letter to the Director of the Corunna Academy, it is very interesting to notice the reiteration of the *Jefe de M.I.R* to his subordinates in the tact and the way he handled the "*negrillos*," because of their different idiosyncrasies and habits:

"...It is my utter interest that you discretely take the greatest care in the closing moments of the course at the Academy that you direct in such a praiseworthy way, so that the *negrillo* instructors be satisfied with the consideration shown to their collaboration as instructors, and not only by you but most particularly by the teachers and students at your orders. Let's measure out their susceptibilities in accordance with ours, and let's avoid criteria of all kinds; when a modifying indication regarding their criteria is necessary, absolutely necessary, let this be done with flair in such a way that it becomes a praise of their initiatives and the modification of that criterion be conditioned by time imperatives, requirements of another discipline or forms of our psychology. It is necessary to recognize our collaborators' goodwill and the exigencies of a political nature that must not escape patriotism and your understanding and that of your collaborators, the teachers of that Academy. The small details that show too much the hallmark of the instructors' idiosyncrasy as an antithesis to our tradition, can be slightly modified, with tact and cleverness, as it happens to be with the waving of the arms as we march; it is my wish that the waving be done on parades, keeping rhythm and very much in accordance with the latter, without exaggeration, but in no way must it be suppressed. I would like to see the development of initiatives aimed at sealing this collaboration with the *negrillo* instructors at the end of the same, so as to make their pride satisfied, in order to facilitate the task of the High Command with the latter and their high leaders, which is required by the conveniences of Spain."

Four courses were given, all of them in Corunna, with a total of 670 automobile sergeants trained.

Academia de Automovilismo **courses**

Course	Notice	Period	Places	Applications	Admitted	Dismissed & unfit	Graduates
1st	16-08-37	20-09 / 20-10	250	626	264	41	223
2nd	None*	17-11 / 16-12	200	680	244	65	179
3rd	31-01-38	01-03 / 29-03	150	700	185	43	142
4th	None*	10-04 / 10-05	150	1,171	172	46	126

* Those dismissed on previous notices were given a second chance

The "*negrillo*" advisers of the Engineers Corps

During the Great War, traditional communications based on the telephone and optical (signal flags, torches, heliograph, etc.) and electric telegraphy were expanded with a new type of equipment; the radio, or wireless telegraphy.

During the campaigns in Africa, the Spanish Army used all these types of transmission equipment, as did the enemy, for Abd-el Krim had radio interception and decoding teams. At that time, and later, besides the signal units of the Engineers Corps, there were the Artillery equipment, so badly needing a liaison between their own units (gun batteries, observation posts, command posts) and the units they supported. This corps had portable Marconi YA 1 radios, and mobile YB 1 radios et al during that war. Also during the Asturias Revolution, the Engineers Corps used mobile radios, such as the CL 10.

In 1936, the obvious political steps that the Republic had made had reduced the communication units to two cores, the *Regimiento de Comunicaciones* at El Pardo, Madrid, whose third Battalion was the only wireless telegraphy unit; and the Army Signals Battalion in Morocco. After the uprising, the former played a leading part on a long march from its quartering to Segovia, as the uprising of the Madrid garrison failed. The obvious consequence was that it had to abandon all the equipment, except for two 100-watt radios, and sustained painful casualties.

In such overall state, it is not surprising that the communications equipment of the early months was minimal; each of the three columns of the *Ejército de África* (Castejón, Asensio and Tella) could hardly count on a radio station, on horseback or vehicles, and heavy optics whereas in the North, *coronel* Beorlegui's had to improvise his, by customizing civil radio manned by personnel of the "*Radio Requeté de Campaña*" (*Requeté*, Field Radio).

Although the personnel and equipment situation gradually improved thanks to strenuous efforts, German and Italian help was always welcome. The framework of the same was the different schools for temporary officers and NCOs, where operation of foreign equipment was taught, and also the specific German training units.

The Temporary Engineers Second Lieutenant Academy (Sappers and Signals) established by the *Jefatura de M.I.R.*, remained in Burgos—in the premises of the La Merced Jesuit Convent, where the *Junta de Defensa* had established it—until the end of the war. It should be reminded that, after the expulsion of this religious order by the Republic, their premises had remained idle. The Perfectioning Academy for Engineers 1st lieutenants

Several "*negrillos*" using a German radio on operations. (via Raúl Arias)

was also based in the same place until June 1938 when it moved to San Sebastian, maybe because in the industrious North, they were closer to the factories producing machines and cording equipment; initially, and for a very short time, it had been in Segovia.

The total number of officers trained was 160 1st lieutenants and nearly 500 2nd lieutenants. As of 1 February 1938, Engineers temporary sergeants were trained in San Sebastian and Saragossa.

The German Signals advisers: *Gruppe Siber*

The first documented evidence of the support of the German instructors to the Engineers academies is recorded in March 1938. Shortly after the establishment of the *Grupo de Instrucción de Artillería* at Monasterio de Rodilla, Burgos, a Mixed Sappers-Miners and Signals Company was also founded and based in Burgos city.

Radio operator at the Artillery School at Monasterio de Rodilla (Burgos).

In the film made by the "*negrillos*" in February 1938 "*Spanien 1938*," several aspects of the training of the field artillery batteries with modern portable radios are shown and, besides, two sequences are very interesting: a radio operator at a radio-direction finder to intercept signals, and another one with an Enigma machine; the latter, although of the so-called commercial type (i. e. not specifically military) were easier to decode, they were certainly accompanied by others, more modern and of the same type, like those preserved now as real relics at the Defense General Staff HQs.

Some more information comes from a proposal of a "*Programa de Instrucción de Telefonía*" (Telephony Training Syllabus) dated at Vinaroz on 6 September 1938, and which was later translated into Spanish in Burgos on 24 December, when Captain Oscar Kohler, of *Gruppe Siber,* established the bases for a three or four-week course, with 25 school days. A list of the equipment regarded as necessary for the same, dated 9 October and drafted at Monasterio de Rodilla, allows one to see that the training on the 1933 model field telephones (*Feldfernsprecher* 33) and their corresponding switchboards, which were to be produced in Spain in postwar, were recommended.

Based on the syllabus above, and once approved by the First Section of the Staff of the C.G.G. on 30 December, two courses were given at the Monasterio Academy, so that the Infantry groups could have their own signals equipment and personnel in order to ensure liaison. The capacity of the signals school was one hundred students per course, which allowed two officers, ten sergeants, and eighty corporals and soldiers to attend to the first course, which started on 15 January 1939. In the second course, which ended by late March, the number of attending troops was seventy.

Colonel Siber, according to what can be seen from the settlement commission records on the *Legión Condor* equipment handed over to Spain at the end of the war, was the head of signals of the German Unit, on whom the rest of the Signals Groups depended technically, both of the *Luftwaffe* and the *Heer*. The teams were concentrated at the *Parque de Comunicaciones* in Valladolid and were used to equip several units of the new post-war Army, including the *Regimiento de Comunicaciones* for the Air Force.

(Authors)

INSTRUCTORS AT THE *ACADEMIA DE COMUNICACIONES* AT MONASTERIO DE RODILLA

NAME	RANK	PERIOD	REMARKS
Kohler, Oscar	Maj	06-38 / 05-39	Chief Instructor. *Escuela de Comunicaciones*
Beuse, Frederich	Sgt	07-38 / 05-39	Instructor. *Escuela de Comunicaciones*
Czerwenka, Ernst	Lt	01-38 / 05-39	Instructor. *Escuela de Comunicaciones*
Dornheim, Wilhelm	NCO	07-38 / 05-39	Instructor. *Escuela de Comunicaciones*
Hoferdt, Gerhardt	1/Lt	03-39 / 05-39	Instructor. *Escuela de Comunicaciones*
Klagge, Heribert	NCO	01-39 / 05-39	Instructor. *Escuela de Comunicaciones*
Petzold, Kurt	1/Lt	01-38 / 05-39	Instructor. *Escuela de Comunicaciones*
Schillinger, Hermann	1/Lt	03-39 / 05-39	Instructor. *Escuela de Comunicaciones*
Seiler, Ludwig	1/Lt	07-37 / 01-39	Instructor
Haendler, Ferdinand	Interpreter	09-37 / 05-39	

German Pioneers-Miners at the *Academia de Engineers*

Regarding the German instructors training on tactics and sapper-miner technique, the first documentary support available is dated 9 March 1938, when both Artillery batteries of the *negrillo* instructors mentioned above and the single Engineers (i.e. sappers) single battery were in Burgos city, the latter certainly collaborating with the Engineers Academy established in the Jesuit convent. It happened that the Engineers equipment was stored at Fuentes Blancas, a forest near the Miraflores charterhouse, far away from the town, for which reason orders were issued to the effect that tactical training, directed by the "*negrillos*," was to be carried out alternatively at this enclave and in the town.

In this field, besides what was stated regarding the flame throwers, one can conjecture that German help stuck to fortification equipment, namely modern mines and barbed wire, all of them elements not unknown to the Spanish military, who had invented the "*carlista* trench" and the "blocao"[34] (discontinued fortification), and who also had the Biosca flame throwers, standard since 1918. Besides, they had experienced the

(J.M. Campesino via Raúl Arias)

(J.M. Campesino via Raúl Arias)

efficiency of the antipersonnel mines and against makeshift armored trucks or "*tiznaos*"[35] of the Rif fighters.

In the summer of 1937, Germany supplied the first T, or Teller, anti-tank mines that were later to be widely used in the Second World War, even by the Spanish *División Azul* soldiers in Russia, and copies of which have been in the arsenals of different armies to the present, such as in the former Yugoslavia. A barbed wire type was also tested in Spain, of the so-called K rapid type; when compressed, it was circle shaped, 20-cm wide, and had a 1-m radius. There is proof of their presence substantiated by documents in the works by our friend Jacinto Arévalo Molina.

ENGINEERS (SAPPERS-MINERS) INSTRUCTORS ACADEMY

NAME	RANK	PERIOD	REMARKS
Thomas, Johannes	Maj		02-38 / 11-38
Chief Instructor *Escuela de Ingenieros*			
Schesmer, Horst	Lt Col	11-38 / 03-39	Chief Instructor *Escuela de Ingenieros*
Junkereit, Gerhard	1/Lt	03-38 / 05-39	Instructor. *Escuela de Ingenieros*
Leonhardt, Frederich	NCO	03-38 / 10-38	Instructor. *Escuela de Ingenieros*
Moeller, Johannes	1/Lt	03-38 / 03-39	Instructor. *Escuela de Ingenieros*
Renners, Anton	1/Lt	03-38 / 03-39	Instructor. *Escuela de Ingenieros*
Romeyke, Heinrich	1/Lt	03-38 / 12-38	Instructor. *Escuela de Ingenieros*
Wolf, Horst	1/Lt	03-38 / 03-39	Instructor. *Escuela de Ingenieros*

16

Other Members of the *Heer* in Spain

So far, we have reviewed all those who, for the purposes of this work, have been seen as "von Thoma's men," i.e. the Germans of the different units who were operationally under Colonel Wilhelm *Ritter* von Thoma's orders.

The men of the tank, anti-tank gun, flame thrower, and workshop training units; the *Falange Española* militia instructors and the temporary Infantry second lieutenant and sergeant academies; the Artillery training Group; Chemical Warfare, Signals, and Sappers, Automobile, mine throwers, or Naval Military School instructors have marched along these pages, all under a common factor, to be under Colonel Thoma's direct orders. But as we pointed out in the introduction, the land contingent of the German Army in Spain, *Gruppe Imker*, was not under von Thoma's orders, but under *Oberstleutnant* Hans *Freiherr* von Funck's. This officer replaced *Oberstleutnant* Walter Warlimont in his functions as "representative of the German Army at the Generalissimo's HQs," and then, after the recognition of Nationalist Spain by his country, as German Military Attaché in Spain. It was then von Funck the German soldier on whom depended all of the *Heer* units that served in the Spanish Civil War.

It is obvious that this work would remain incomplete if we did not mention, even in a brief way—for the relevant information is very rare and fragmentary—the rest of the *Heer* units that took part in the Spanish conflict, without a direct dependence on von Thoma, but incorporated into von Funck's *Gruppe Imker*. These were, on the one

Oberstleutnant Hans Freiherr von Funck was the head of *Gruppe Imker*. He was also the Military Attaché in Salamanca (via Raúl Arias)

hand, the *Imker Stab* itself, i.e. of the German contingent staff; and on the other hand, the intelligence units of the group, the so-called *Horchtruppen* or radio monitoring troops, as well as the so-called *Imker Ic.*, Intelligence section of the land contingent incorporated into the unit staff itself.

Gruppe Imker Staff

Like any other military unit, no matter how small, *Gruppe Imker* established a staff, directly dependent on its head, *Oberstleutnant* von Funck. With an unknown personnel list, but which might well be around thirty or forty men, commanded by a captain, the Group Staff was based in Salamanca, and similar to the liaison officers at the Generalissimo's HQs, the *Jefatura de M.I.R.*, and other large Spanish and Italian units, it had the typical Personnel, Operations, and Intelligence sections.

The data we have managed to gather, as explained above, are very partial and practically unconnected, although we have indeed managed to trace the names of about twenty members who were at one time or another part of the so-called *Imker Stab*:

(via Francisco Marin)

MEMBERS OF THE *IMKER STAB**

NAME	RANK	ARRIVED	REMARKS
Von Funck, Hans	Col	09-36	*Imker* CO
Wilhelmi	,	Maj	?
Liaison officer at the C.G.G.			
Weltner, Wulf	Capt	?	
Ulich, Heinrich		Capt	12-02-38
Rohbach, Jurgen	1/Lt	27-01-38	
Hennig, Helmuth	2/Lt	?	
Skorzewski, Lothar	2/Lt	27-01-38	
Wolff, Herbert	W/O	07-03-38	
Brand, Wilhelm	W/O	02-04-38	
von Gross, Heinz-Ulrich	W/O	27-01-38	
Hillmann, Albin	W/O	27-01-38	
Draeger, Walter	W/O	27-01-38	
Werner, Rolf	W/O	27-01-38	
Mannigel, Walter	W/O	27-01-38	
Rauchfuss, Helmuth	W/O	27-01-38	
Meyer, Oskar	W/O	?	Killed in car crash 29-03-37
Felkkoetter, Heinrich	Sgt	14-02-38	
Geisel, Karl	Sgt	14-02-38	
Killed at Bujaraloz 25-03-38			
Kunzelmann, Johannes	Sgt	14-02-38	
Wiegand, Paul	Sgt	14-02-38	
Wolfahrt,	Otto	Sgt	14-02-38
Nauck, Herbert	Interpreter	12-02-38	
Fehdmer,	Walter	Interpreter	12-02-38
Mensing,	Guido	Interpreter	12-02-38

* The list is incomplete. Only the *Stab* members that were in Spain for certain are recorded here. About 80/90 men may have served in the unit during the whole war.

(Juan Arráez)

Intelligence section advisers: ***Imker Ic.***

When the *Legión Cóndor* was officially established in the first week of November 1936, an enigmatic "business" called Bureau Linde was also founded on the first floor at no 4, Espoz and Mina Street in Salamanca.

This name, *Bureau Linde* (Linde Office in English), was actually a cover name of what we could refer to as the intelligence service of the German unit, and was maintained until the 11 February of the following year, when this most important service changed its name "...for internal questions..."—as recorded on the note sent to the C.G.G.—to be known from then on as "*Legión Cóndor S.I.M.*"[36]

It was the main intelligence service of the *Legión Cóndor*, although we have traced documents that use different designations to refer to this service called *Sander Ic.* (Sander was the cover name of *General* Sperrle, first commander of the *Legión Cóndor*) or S/88 Ic./SIM, under *Oberstleutnant* Riemschneider's orders. There were also other "offices," e.g. the so-called *Bureau Grau*, the liaison office of the German S.I.M. in Salamanca, under *Oberstleutnant* Grau's orders, or the so-called *Sorau Ic.*

Similarly, one of the sections of the land contingent Staff, i.e. of *Gruppe Imker*, was also the so-called *Imker Ic.*, which sent periodical reports to the HQs Office of the Group and to the Nationalist military authorities.

The establishment of all these intelligence services is contemporary of the establishment of the units they belonged to, and their operations, despite the logical imperfections under the given circumstances, were generally highly regarded by the recipients of the information.

The captain CO of the *Gruppe Wolm*, with a radio operator operating a directional antenna of one of the monitoring teams.

Close-up of the radio operator in the previous picture. The monitoring equipment supplied by the German radio interception company was highly sophisticated.

Imker-Horch Kompanie: **Gruppe *Wolm***

According to Domingo Pastor Petit ("*Los Dossiers secretos de la Guerra Civil*," Argos Vergara), "...the *Legión Cóndor* intelligence service did not start operations in Spain until early November 1936. (...) The *Legión Cóndor* monitoring section, of which the *Imker Horch* was in charge, intercepted, analyzed and decrypted a large amount of Republican messages. The results were sent to the SIPM in Burgos...."

Indeed, one of the least known units in the *Legión Cóndor* field is the special radio-monitoring unit of the *Heer*, the so-called *Imker Horch-Kompanie*. Very little is known about this unit, for its participation in the Spanish Civil War was surrounded by most strict confidentiality, both regarding its operation and its daily reports for the different units. Let's first see the background of their use in pre-war Germany.

Origins of radio monitoring units in Germany

The *Reichswehr* paid great attention to everything related to signals intelligence. Each division had a signals battalion (*Nachriten Abteilung*, NA) with two companies, each with four sections. One of these eight sections, namely no. 4 of the 2 NA Company, was called the *Horchzug*, i.e. the monitoring section. On the other hand, in different border garrisons there were interception detachments at the disposal of the signals commanders of the strongholds (*Festen Horchstellen*).

In order to improve coordination between the operational and static units of the strongholds regarding procedures, teams, etc., links were established between the different communication battalions and the different *Festen Horchstellen*.

Checking overhead lines. (Javier del Campo collection)

The interception section of the NA of the 1. Division was working in contact with the *Festen Horchstellen* of Königsberg, that of the 2. Division did so with that of Stettin, that of the 3. Division did so with those of Spandau, Breslau, Liegnitz, and Frankfurt-am-Oder, that of the 4. Division did so with that of Dresden, that of the 5. Division did so with those of Stuttgart and Kassel, that of the 6. Division did so with those of Hanover and Munster, and that of the 7. Division did so with that of Munich.

By the early 1930s, in each Division Staff the signals officer (*Stabsoffizier Nachrichten*, *Stonach* for short) had three officers at his disposal: an officer responsible for personnel and organization of the communication networks, a technical officer responsible for teams and equipment, and an officer responsible for the interception services, which gives us an idea of the importance of radio monitoring.

As Hitler grabbed power, the German Armed Forces began a quick expansion process that certainly affected communications, including the interception services. One of the changes was the establishment of signals units at Army Corps or Army level, and another one was that for the first time *Horchtruppen* units were established at company level.

In August 1935 the *Versuchs-Horchskompanie* (Experimental Monitoring Company) was established at the Army Signals School. Two months later, in October, the first four *Funk Horch Kompanie* (Radio Monitoring Companies) were established, to be assigned as third companies to a similar number of division signals battalions. One year later a similar unit was established in Düsseldorf.

Two years later, in November 1938, a further two companies of the same type were established, but now they were not attached to divisions anymore, but were battalions specifically created for monitoring missions, with one at Glauchau and another one in Stuttgart.

As these units were established, the Inspector of the Army Signal troops, *General* Fellgiebel, succeeded in changing what until that moment was known as the *Heeres Funkaufklärung* (Army Radio Reconnaissance Service) into the *Horchdienst* (Monitoring Service), and got it consolidated as a *Spezialdienst* (Special Service) within the Signals service. This new classification allowed paying greater attention to its teams, tasks, etc., as well as to determine the operational procedures required to coordinate its missions with those of the Military Intelligence service (*Abwher*).

Evidence of the importance attached to the new units is that the *Nachrichten Lehr und Versuchs Abteilung* (Training and Test Section), assigned to the Signals School in Halle, was made up of three companies: telephony (*Fspre.Kp.*), radio (*Fu.Kp.*), and monitoring (*Fu. Horch. Kp.*).

3. *Fu.Horch. Kp./ Nachr. Abt.* 3, Potsdam
3. *Fu.Horch. Kp./ Nachr. Abt.* 7 Munich
3. *Fu.Horch. Kp./ Nachr. Abt.* 9, Hofgeismar
3. *Fu.Horch. Kp./ Nachr. Abt.* 18, Liegnitz
3. *Fu.Horch. Kp./ Nachr. Abt.* 26, Düsseldorf

The *Horch-Kompanie* of *Gruppe Imker*

There are very few documents of this unit of the land contingent of the *Legión Cóndor* as their operation was always surrounded by great secrecy both by the Germans and the Nationalist authorities. The truth is that the first information unveiled on a radio-monitoring unit refers to it as *Gruppe Korn* and is dated 1 March 1937. It is a report on a radio control duty by that unit, and most probably Korn was at its head at that moment. Another report signed by Korn himself on 17 March warning the Italian mission on the setting up of a French radio station in Algiers to intercept the main transmitter of the Fascist legation placed this officer in Vigo, although the fact is that the document in question has the "*Sander Ic.*" letterhead, which is quite misleading. Probably *Gruppe Korn* was part of the *Legión Cóndor Stab* and had nothing to do with the *Horch-Kompanie* of *Gruppe Imker*.

The truth is that the *Imker* radio-interception company was codenamed *Gruppe Wolm*. As was the case with the rest of the groups established by the *Heer* in Spain (*Gruppe Thoma, Gruppe Issendorff, Gruppe Lucht...*), this unit was called after the name of the first CO upon arrival in Spain. Something similar happened years later when the *División Azul* joined the *Wehrmacht* on its fight on the Soviet Union. The Spanish regiments were named after their colonels' names, i.e. *Regimiento "Pimentel," Regimiento "Rodrigo,"* etc.

Bottom: Close-up of the radio operator in the previous picture. The monitoring equipment supplied by the German radio interception company was highly sophisticated. (Authors)

An Enigma coding machine of the commercial type, used by *Gruppe Wolm* in Spain. (Authors)

The monitoring unit operated in the front areas where there was more important enemy activity, and its main object it was to deduce the enemy deployment and the operation of the command chains out of the interception of radio and telephony signals, with a very special interest in detecting Republican offensive intentions.

The officers responsible for intelligence signals depended on the "*Ic.*" officers (who were the HQs and Staff intelligence head officers), who told them which sector or sectors should be watched more closely. Most of the radio interception task was aimed at intercepting signals of the lower echelons (at battalion or regimental level), which were the easiest ones to decode, paying special attention to the communications network of the Republican artillery and the armored units. Nevertheles, perfect control was also maintained on communications of the brigades and divisions of the *Ejército Popular de la República* (People's Army of the Republic, EPR for short), as well as on other bodies, like the Republican Fleet, the Air Raid Control Network, or the General HQs of the EPR.

The *Horch-Kompanie* that operated in Spain was commanded by a captain and was made up of three sections, each commanded by a 1st lieutenant, which operated independently and at different places in the Nationalist territory.

Each section had the necessary means to intercept enemy intelligence, with monitoring specialists on long and short wave emissions, telephony, and even telegraphy.

In order to give an idea of the modus operandi of the unit, two résumés of the monitoring services carried out by the CO 1st lieutenant of the so-called East Section of *Gruppe Wolm* in October 1937 are quoted (see pp 199-200).

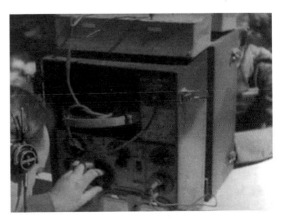

German radio operator. (Authors)

Group Wolm   Saragossa, 16 October 1937
      East Section   II Triumphant Year

Nº 15 (15 October 1937) Service duties Résumé

Long Wave: Nothing to report
Short Wave: *Ejército del Este* Network:

This network was on intense control duties as usual. Nine telegrams were intercepted in plain text, the contents of which were irrelevant. The heading of these telegrams allowed locating the HQs of the following *Brigadas*:

133 Brigada at Sasa de Abadiado (confirmation), *144 Brigada* at Calanda (Teruel)
Besides, the Engineers General Commander residence was placed in Lérida.
Station 's2' was called several times today by several stations, had no reply. At 0310 hrs 'ts1' (XII *Cuerpo de Ejército* at Alcañiz) says to 'ts3', "Tell me why 'ts2' does not reply." 'ts3' answers, "It surely is under repair, has not replied for several days" ('ts2' was heard here even on 14.10. Nothing heard on the 15th). On 15.10, several calls from 'hp3' (*Carlos Marx* Div.) to "hp1" were heard again, sounds strange that the latter is not heard here.

Air Raid Control Network

This network was again on intense control duties, also sending alarm reports, which have not been decoded yet. At 1820 hrs "cxd" station called a new station, "ffc", for the first time. The latter could not be monitored.

Complementary Networks:

As regards these networks, it is striking that only stations 'em 1', 'em 16' and 'em 61', belonging to the 'em' network were observed today. (New observations, see first paragraph of Telephony this résumé)

Telephony:

'Central' station (75 m) and stations 'em3' (62 m) and 'd3' (62 m) were observed on mutual control duties. After the control duties between these stations, it transpires that the 'd' network and the "em" network stations are in direct communication with the central station. Besides, "central" station called station 'd2', had no reply.

On 1 January 1937 the Reds introduced a change, a "ring" of stations on Telephony with the specific purpose of passing on, on prearranged turns, the war reports from the different fronts and, besides, last minute news, both military and political. For that purpose the most powerful stations were picked up, but that ring was eventually a failure and was cancelled shortly afterwards.

Now, and apparently with the same purpose to start on 16 October a new ring under the direction of station 'si 1' from Valencia, according to a report from that same station on 15.10.37 at 1640 h, and says, "In order that the ring runs smoothly tomorrow and officially as homage to the heroic Asturias, the following change is to be introduced, after 'r7', 'r8', comes Gijón and later the Asturias "cnt" and then the others in the ring." In addition, the 'Republican fleet' station, "Received, 'popular front' will appear on the córdoba (sic) front. Make it sure that '1 dd' (26 *División*) is not out because it is loud and clear."

The following stations of that network were heard on 15-10-37, 'si 1' Valencia, 'Valencia traffic', 'Madrid 9 radio', 'republican fleet', 'r8' and 'north radio'. However, we have not managed to observe the stations mentioned by the ones above in their control duties, 'si4' (Raca?) 'r7', 'pc2' (communist party, Gijón), Asturias 'cnt', '1 dd' and 'fpm2' (Cordoba front)

'Mobile' and 'c' stations were on control duties. As it is known, these two networks are on the front between Calamocha and Teruel.

                                                    Lieutenant and Head of East Section

Group Wolm   Saragossa, 18 October 1937
East Section   II Triumphant Year

N° 17 (17 October 1937) Service duties Resumee

Long Wave: Nothing to report
Short Wave: *Ejército del Este* Network:

This network was as usual on internal control duties. Control duties between stations 'ts48' (Lérida) and 'era' (Ministry of Defence, Valencia) were observed again. Besides station 'ts48' sent a control call to station "ege" (Barcelona).
At 1555 hrs station 'ts2', which had been unserviceable for two days, was again on duty. The latter called 'ts6' (Head of the *Ejército del Este* in Lérida) on control.

Air Raid Control Network

This network did not do much on control duties and just sent some telegrams. These telegrams just gave orders to dismantle some stations. These are orders from the central of that 'ffa' network (Candasnos) to 7 Air Raid Alarm stations, which were ordered to report at the Lérida airfield with observers and stations.
As of 1545 hrs this network ceased operations, so a complete reorganization of this network is to be expected.

Telephony:
Short Wave: Stations 'hp1' and 'hp3' (*Carlos Marx* Div.) were observed on control duties. A telegram was intercepted in plain text, the contents of which were irrelevant.
The "ring" was observed, control service duties between some stations were intercepted.
     On the 43.5-m band 'mobile 1' station was observed on control duties with station '25 Div.' At 1410 hrs '25 Div.' says to 'mobile 1',: "hallo, mobile 1 of 25 *División*, 25 Div. on the Aragon front is calling you." From this, it can be deduced that the 25 *División* must have several "mobile" stations on the Aragon front, apparently belonging to the brigades.
     At 1555 hrs *25 Div.* also says to 'mobile 1', "Listen, if you have something to tell me, do so in 'graph', for which reason, beside the telephony service they must have a telegraphy service. Besides, the *25 Div.* and *26 Div.* stations were observed on mutual control duties. The staff stations of the 'mobile' and 'c' networks were observed on the usual duties.

1ª Lieutenant and Head of East Section

It is obvious that the experience gained by *Gruppe Wolm* in the Spanish Civil War was of great value, and was an inflexion point in the development of the *Wehrmacht* radio monitoring units. This experience was the key to combat use of these special German units, who proved their real importance for the development of military operations during the Second World War.

Rommel had one of the most efficient intelligence signal units of the German Army, the 3. (*Fu. Horch. Kp*)/*Nachr Abt* 56. The first detachment of this company arrived in Libya on 25 February 1941. It was a section under the orders of 1/Lt Gerisch. It was not until 24 April that the company was in full strength on African soil, with 1/Lt Seebohm as its CO.

During 1940-1941 la 3.(*Fu.Horch. Kp*)/*Nachr Abt* 56 had been deployed in Le Havre to carry out radio reconnaissance on England.

Seebohm was one of the best German specialists on the subject. According to Piekalkiewicz, the work of this company and that of its CO was "Rommel's most reliable intelligence source." With great agility, the company specialists were able to determine the deployment of enemy troops, and the form of that deployment allowed them to deduce the operational (offensive or defensive) intentions of the enemy.

Seebohm's company—which at some time became *Nachrichten Funkaufklärungs Kompanie* 621 (NFK 621), i.e. 621 Radio Scout Company—was made up of two echelons: the first one, with the company Staff and one of the sections, stayed by Rommel's HQs. It was in charge of decoding and evaluating all the signals intercepted. A second echelon, with the sections in charge of interception, was deployed in the operations area. Every important message was sent to the first echelon, decoded, and forwarded to Rommel. Among the company personnel, whose average was 25 years old and had a good command of English, message-decoding specialists were vital.

The company made daily résumés of their activity and a monthly résumé of all the information intercepted, just like they had done in the Spanish Civil War.

The British eventually found out that NFK 621 was one of their worst enemies. During the Battle of El Alamein their emplacement was detected at Tell el Aisa, very close to the coast. On the night of 9 to 10 July 1942 a local offensive was mounted with three battalions which crossed the positions of an Italian division with the purpose of finishing off Seebohm's unit. The attack was a success for the British, as Seebohm and his second in command, 1/Lt Herz, were captured, along with seventy-one other members of the company, which was a hard blow, as the British had hold of all the equipment of the unit.

According to Piekalkiewicz, "it was that attack that sealed the fate of the Battle of El Alamein later, for from then on Rommel was unaware of the enemy plans."

Oberleutnant Hertzer was the CO of *Gruppe Wolm*. (Authors)

GRUPPE WOLM* MEMBERS

NAME	RANK	ARRIVAL DATE
Adam, Otto	Sgt	-
Bachner, Maxim	Sgt	01/01/1938
Ballentin, Harry	Sgt	01/01/1938
Barnickel, Otto	Sgt	01/01/1938
Basner, Oskar	Sgt	01/01/1938
Bauer, Johannes	Sgt	01/01/1938
Becker, Walter	Sgt	01/01/1938
Bex, Heinrich	Sgt	-
Binder, Johannes	Sgt	-
Birkenbeul, Rudolf	W/O	30/10/1937
Blumenfeld, Alfred	Interpreter	22/02/1937
Bogner, Adolf	W/O	-
Brockschmidt, Jurgen	Sgt	01/01/1938
Bull, Wolfgang	Sgt	-
Clauss, Richard	Sgt	-
Czerwenka, Ernst	2/Lt	07/03/1938
Dreischer, Otto	2/Lt	-
Duenninger, Oswald	Sgt	26/10/1937
Eckstein, Werner	W/O	-
Ehrenberg, Erik	Sgt	-
Farob, Harald	Sgt	03/11/1937
Favoro, Dietrich	Sgt	03/11/1937
Fehrentz, Ernst	Sgt	-
Feichtner, Ferdinand	1/Lt	19/01/1938
Frappe, Rudolf	Intelligence	26/10/1937
Frey, Karl	W/O	26/10/1937
Frey, Frederich	Sgt	-
Fritsche, Günther	Sgt	01/01/1938
Garbe, Helmuth	Sgt	-
Golder, Johannes	Sgt	01/01/1938
Gratins, Erik	W/O	12/01/1938
Grotz, Walter	1/Lt	18/02/1938
Gruen, Heinrich	Sgt	12/01/1938
Hassloerver, Johannes	Sgt	03/11/1937
Henne, Frederich	Sgt	01/01/1938
Hillner, Frederich	Sgt	01/01/1938
Hofbauer, Joseph	Sgt	
Hoffmann, Bruno	Sgt	-
Huhn, Bruno	Sgt	-
Jansen, Joseph	W/O	-
Kaempfer, Hermann	2/Lt	-
Kaettner, Otto	Sgt	-
Kahlert, Erdhard	W/O	-
Kahn, Maxim	Capt	08/11/1937
Kaminski, Rudolf	W/O	19/01/1938
Kaul, Werner	Sgt	-
Kaulen, Walter	Sgt	-
Kiefer, Karl	Military official	-
Kirchhoff, Johannes	Sgt	03/11/1937
Klamm, Erich	Sgt	03/11/1937
Klein, Rudi	Sgt	-
Klein, Karl	Sgt	03/11/1937

NAME	RANK	ARRIVAL DATE
Koehler, Frederich	Sgt	03/11/1937
Koerner, Lothar	Sgt	-
Kolada, Paul	2/Lt	21/10/1937
Krieger, Frederich	Sgt	03/11/1937
Kuhn, Gerhard	Sgt	21/10/1937
Lebrecht, Carl	Sgt	01/01/1938
Leppin, Rudolf	Sgt	01/01/1938
Leps, Wilhelm	Sgt	-
Lettl, Joseph	Sgt	-
Littheim, Rudolf	Sgt	21/10/1937
Loeffer, Alfred	W/O	26/10/1937
Ludwig, Wilhelm	W/O	26/10/1937
Maass, Sigfred	W/O	26/10/1937
Maerker, Horst	Sgt	-
Manger, Johannes	Sgt	-
Meister, Albert	Sgt	-
Merkel, Frederich	Sgt	-
Mischon, Richard	Sgt	01/01/1938
Morgenstern, Frederich	Sgt	-
Mueller, Kurt	Sgt	01/01/1938
Mueller, Herbert	2/Lt	07/03/1938
Mueller, Jurgen	Sgt	21/10/1937
Naegele, Erwin	Sgt	21/10/1937
Neunzig, Felix	Interpreter	-
Niederreiter, Kurt	2/Lt	-
Ockert, Bruno	Sgt	01/01/1938
Oertel, Johannes	Sgt	01/01/1938
Olislagers, Paul	Sgt	12/02/1938
Petzold, Kurt	2/Lt	07/03/1938
Pfleiderel, Wilhelm	Sgt	01/01/1938
Pfumfel, Gerhard	Sgt	-
Pieper, Albert	Sgt	-
Piwonka, Kurt	Interpreter	-
Plass, Carlos	Sgt	22/02/1937
Ploetner, Maxim	W/O	01/01/1938
Poenninghaus, Heinrich	Sgt	01/01/1938
Poepping, Frederich	Sgt	-
Reich, Bernhard	Sgt	21/10/1937
Reiher, Frederich	Sgt	21/10/1937
Richner, Hermann	2/Lt	01/01/1938
Roemmling, Paul	2/Lt	-
Roesler, Walther	Sgt	03/11/1937
Rogge, Heinz	2/Lt	07/03/1938
Ruster, Reinald	Sgt	03/11/1937
Sansen, August	Sgt	26/10/1937
Schäfer, Johannes	W/O	-
Schlender, Horst	Sgt	03/11/1937
Schletter, Gerhard	Sgt	26/10/1937
Schmitt, Heinrich	Sgt	03/11/1937
Schmitt, Maxim	Sgt	03/11/1937
Schneider, Franz	Sgt	-
Schoelich, Jurgen	Sgt	21/10/1937
Schol, Walter	Sgt	03/11/1937

NAME	RANK	ARRIVAL DATE
Scholtz, Benito	Sgt	-
Schoor, Alfred	Sgt	-
Schroeder, August	Sgt	12/01/1938
Schuffenhaner, German	Interpreter	21/10/1937
Schurr, Johannes	Sgt	01/01/1938
Seegers, Otto	Sgt	-
Seidel, Alfred	Sgt	-
Seliger, Alfred	Sgt	01/01/1938
Spernal, Ruppert	Sgt	-
Sppinger, Ludt	Sgt	26/10/1937
Stegmir, Peter	W/O	21/10/1937
Stief, Walter	2/Lt	07/03/1938
Strauss, Kurt	Sgt	-
Stroesser, Joseph	Sgt	01/01/1938
Umbreit, Karl	Sgt	01/01/1938
von Voedtke, Jurgen	Interpreter	22/02/1937
Voeringer, Karl	Sgt	03/11/1937
Voese, Walter	Sgt	26/10/1937
Vollrath, Karl	Interpreter	-
Wanner, Frederich	Sgt	01/01/1938
Wegschneider, Franz	Sgt	-
When, Karl	Sgt	03/11/1937
Weiglin, Gerhard	Sgt	-
Will, Robert	Sgt	01/01/1938
Wissmann, Joachim	W/O	-
Witte, Heinrich	W/O	-
Worm, Otto	W/O	-
Wusterkans, Willi	1/Lt	08/11/1937
Wysocki, Alfred	NCO	-
Zeller, Robert	Sgt	-
Ziegler, Frederich	Sgt	-

* The list is incomplete. It includes the members of the *Gruppe Wolm* that were in Spain for certain. About 180 or 200 men may have served in the unit along the whole war

Casualties of the *Horch-Kompanie* of *Gruppe Imker*

Gruppe Wolm had four casualties in the Spanish conflict; although none was killed in action, two were killed in accidents, one committed suicide, and another one died of natural causes. It is not confirmed that another two, Sgt Mayer and interpreter Paege, belonged to *Gruppe Wolm*, but there are sound signs that they did. Despite the doubts, they are included in this list.

NAME	RANK	DATE	CAUSE &PLACE
Börflet, Hans	Radio operator	29/09/38	Typhus, Saragossa
Hübner, Willy	Interpreter	15/12/38	Truck crash, Saragossa
Mayer, Oskar	Sgt	29/03/37	Car crash, San Martín de Valdeiglesias
Noack, Kurt	Radio operator	06/08/37	Truck crash, Lomilla, Palencia
Paege, Wilhelm	Interpreter	03/03/38	Pneumonia, Burgos
Seifert, Helmuth	Radio operator	22/09/38	Suicide, Saragossa

Appendix 1:
The Toledo Officers Academy,
Instructors "Otto" and "Fritz"

Some chapters of José María Gárate Córdoba's magnificent book *Mil días de fuego*,[37] published by Luis de Caralt, Barcelona, portray daily life at the *Academia de Tenientes Provisionales* in Toledo in a masterful way. The German instructors nicknamed "Otto" and "Fritz" are often mentioned there.

In order to give a better idea of the daily life with the German instructors at those schools, we are excerpting here the most curious aspects mentioned in that chapter:

"...The suitcases had to be left and we had to go downstairs quickly. There we met the first German, a photographer warrant officer who had planned everything, and welcomed us 'on the wait,' as we came down, like the hunter haunts his prey. In groups, he took photographs of us in fours on the steps, two in kneeling position and two standing behind (...)

(...) But the real novelty came from the German instructors. At the start we didn't like them at all, neither 'Otto' nor 'Fritz.' From the very beginning, the easy nickname from the jokes in vogue stuck to these two captains of the tactical companies. And they quite suited them because they corresponded to very different biotypes. 'Fritz' was rather athletic and Prussian, with a stiff face and a toy soldier walk. 'Otto' was ours, an apoplexy pyknic, a euphoric tubby Bavarian, surely a good tankard drinker, who went red hot, both to laugh and tear a strip off and at the slightest hint of ridicule. I think nobody knew anything about his previous life, but on the third day the rumor went around that he was one of those razor blade salesmen who used to go round the province fairs before the war, praising the excellent qualities of his Solingen steel blades, 'for hard beard *und* for soft beard,' who made the test of a dry shave for free to the first patient ready to suffer it and then they gave him a ten-blade set. According to the know-it-alls, they were Hitlerite spies, temporary second or first lieutenants—with white stars—promoted one or two ranks above as they joined the active service.

Everything was new: the composition, the tactics and command. Here came 1/ Lt 'Pencil,' who, according to those in the know, was a professional lieutenant and an aristocrat. The 'Pencil' nickname clearly originated in his shape, with a pointed head under that tall stiff cap which added him what was needed to reach six feet. He made us stand at attention in that strange way, with bow-shaped arms, with the index finger ends on the trouser seams and the hand backs facing forwards and reviewed us. Right in time, chronometric, came the Captain, he saluted and said,

'Good morning, First Company!'

A unanimous choir, with excessive enthusiasm, shouted back,

'Good morning, Captain!'

New to us also that 112-step, nearly redoubled, and singing on marching full step, in serious mood, no matter how humorous the songs were. Well, Prussian humor at its best. These were translated German songs, to which we added the suitable native tone with a thick nasal voice:

The cadets march
in correct formation
and girls runnn
to the balcooo...ny (...)

(...) The '*On the run, march!*' was another German invention which only had a slight change on the phonetic rhythm of our standard voice, '*On the run, march!*' and the Germans used it as a punishment too, replacing our '*nimble step.*' Another common voice, even stranger, was that of '*full deck!*,' equivalent to Spanish *lie down!* It was good for all: to hide from aircraft, artillery and even to punish any collective offense with frequent and sparingly exercise practice.

Those German officers were masters in many trades: for example, in the designation of objectives, making them unmistakable and easy to find first time, although we pretended not to notice, purporting Teutonic mental slowness, which the instructor did not find strange. And this was because it was very funny to hear him repeating his rather comic pronunciation of the few place words they always used: 'On ze left rafine and on ze right rafine. Target: ze little tree zat is shaped like a brush near ze farmhouse.'

Captain 'Otto' was angry every day with the impetuosity of temporary officers, with the common recklessness of the Spanish soldier, 'An officer valking heading his troop does not command, and alzough he might die a hero's death, he leavez them orphan.' I don't know where he had found out those days that there was a battalion on the Teruel front that had five officers and four troop casualties. That was a fine mess they'd had us into!

That morning good 'Otto' time and again got back to his hobbyhorse, forgetting the tactical exercise, 'Zis iz unacceptable! Zis iz suicide! Zis vay you vill be left vizout officers in a month!' Then, in a simple example of advance under fire, he got excited again and shouted, 'You can't crawl! You do it all vildly! You are brave, but bravely dead!' and shooting his finger, he ordered over half the company, which, according to him was at the enemy's mercy, unprotected: 'Oh! Spanish confidence in improvisation is harmful!' to report dead. A few days later we proved him wrong. He was only partly right.

Because of his cycloid temperament, he quickly changed from anger to elation and back. Deep down, he was good-natured, always efficient, but as naïf as a boy. He fought in vain our habit of keeping our hands in our trouser pockets: 'Listen sir! Pick zat stone!' he crouched down to pick it up from the ground and give it to the offender: 'You vill hold it until you find some else vith his hands in his pockets.' Quite often the pebble used to go from hand to hand the whole company with the watchword *Pass it on!* And the last one threw it away after looking at it unenthusiastically. But then a better idea was found. The one who was punished watched carefully until the captain had his handkerchief out of his pocket, caught him in the act and gave him the stone,

'I'm sorry Captain, but orders are orders.'

'Otto' took the prank with a smile. Now he got it first time.

'All right, sir. No exceptions made on duty *und* no one forgiven. (...)'

(...) There were other German instructors, even more models for specialties. They were wonderful. They excelled at everything, at throwing grenades, at busting tanks from deep pits, without perma nor parapet, not the slightest relief, because that which was dug out was hidden somewhere else; at using weapons, perfect, admirable. Hand grenades, German stick grenades, they were fantastic because they had a handle.

These Germans liked war ruses, raids, infiltrations and ambushes very much. (...)

(...) We used to leave and come back singing. We found those songs translated from German rather stupid, having Spanish ones, so plentiful and of our taste. Captain 'Otto' knew and tried not to mortify us too much, and ordered to alternate ones and others

'On ze fourth step, '*El novio de la Muegte*'[38]. One, two, three *und* four.
-'On ze fourth step, '*Anna Marí, ha, ha...*'

But as soon as we had walked a hundred yards, '*El burro de las lecheras*'[39] and other cheekier, even brutal tunes welled up.

Everything was less bad in our company, but 'Fritz' was a more inflexible and inscrutable man, more German, which meant 'squarehead' to us. One day his company decided to go on strike on the German song for some of the Captain's decisions that the students judged unacceptable. Every day in turn, a student took command of the company in closed order, and that day it was Enrique del Real's. Captain 'Fritz,' in a low voice, suggested the song that was due: '*El cogue cogue...*'[40]. Del Real played dumb and shouted,

'On the fourth step, '*Chaparrita*'[41]. One, two, three and four...'

And so on. Things were going from bad to worse. Now they didn't sing in German or in Spanish, and 'Fritz' had them arrested, keeping the company attention for a long time or with long runs. One day he started an individual coercion offensive. He started with Alfonso Pérez Enedáguila, who seemed suited to him,

'You, sir, are not singing.'
'No, Captain.'
'Why?'
'Because my voice is horrible.'

And he had him arrested.

It was bad business for the Germans, because on the way back from training the German colonel, a training inspector or something, used to wait at the academy gate to see us marching in, singing their songs, which caused him great satisfaction. Those of us in 'Otto' made a common cause with those of 'Fritz,' and that day we fell silent as we marched in. Fortunately, the German Colonel was not there, maybe because he had some hint of the undercurrent. (...)

Appendix 2:

Appendix 3:

Cuartel General del Generalísimo   **Estado Mayor**

TELEGRAMA . POSTAL

Sección . TERCERA .

Núm . 1414

Burgos, 20 de Abril de 193 8 .   II Año Triunfal

EL GENERALISIMO

AL GENERAL DIRECTOR DE MOVILIZACION, INSTRUCCION Y RE-
CUPERACION.-   P L A Z A

    Para recompensar la labor de Instrucción desarro-
llada por el Coronel "Negrillo" Von Thoma y personal
que le secundó en su tarea, así como al personal "Legionario" que ha desarrollado análoga labor en bene-
ficio de nuestras Unidades especialistas, se servirá
V.E. formular propuesta razonada de todo el personal
que, a su juicio, deba ser premiado, independiente-
mente de los servicios de guerra propiamente dichos
que será objeto de otras propuestas por las Autoridades competentes.
    Estas propuestas serán independientes por nacio-
nalidades, y para que sirva de orientación por lo
que a Negrillos se refiere, se envía copia resumida
de la labor de Instrucción desarrollada por el Grupo
de Von Thoma desde 1º de octubre de 1936 al mes de
marzo próximo pasado.
    De Orden de S.E.
    El General Jefe de E. M.

ARCHIVO GENERAL MILITAR DE AVILA
(Valleepín, 19 - 05001 AVILA)
Reproducción tomada del original de esta Sección

ARCHIVO GENERAL MILITAR DE AVILA
(Valleepín, 19 - 05001 AVILA)
Reproducción tomada del original de esta Sección

Appendix 4:

Respaldo que se cita.

Material a cargo.

Renault .... 34.
Negrillos .... 84.
Cañon .... 70.

TOTAL 188

Conductores y tiradores con que cuenta.	Conct.	Tirad.
Reemplazo 1.929 y anteriores	10	15
" 1.930 a 1.935	111	89
" 1.935 a 1.941	143	175.

TANTO A LA SEGUNDA SECCIÓN:

    Ante la eventualidad del licenciamiento de
gran parte del personal que presta sus servicios en la Agrupación de Carros de Combate, el Jefe de la misma expresa la con-
veniencia de que se celebre en Casarrubielos un curso de conductores y tiradores al que podrían asistir 200 de cada
clase.
    Al respaldo figura nota del personal y mate-
rial existente, del que se deduce que si sucesivamente se
tributaran los licenciamientos hasta el reemplazo de 1.935 queda-
ría una insuficiencia de conductores y tiradores, hecho que se
pasa a conocimiento de esa Sección por si estimase procedente
aceptar la propuesta del referido Jefe, el cual informa que en
la Escuela de Casarrubielos, y alojado el personal en Cubas y
Casarrubielos, pueden instruirse 70 conductores para Carros
"Negrillos" 50 conductores Carros "Fickers", 70 tiradores "Negrillos" y 50 tiradores "Fickers"; en total 120 conductores y
120 tiradores.
    Independiente de la Escuela, pueden prepa-
rarse personal y material para instruir en el 1º Batallón 120
conductores y 120 tiradores, así como igual número en el 2º Batallón.
    La instrucción del 1º Batallón podría desa-
rrollarse en Alcalá y la del 2º Batallón en Campamento de Cara-
banchel, actuales bases provisionales de los mismos. Ruego me
comunique su resolución.
    Burgos, 12 de Mayo de 1.939
    "AÑO DE LA VICTORIA"

EL TENIENTE CORONEL JEFE DE LA 1ª SECCIÓN,

Appendix 5:
Organization of *Gruppe Imker*

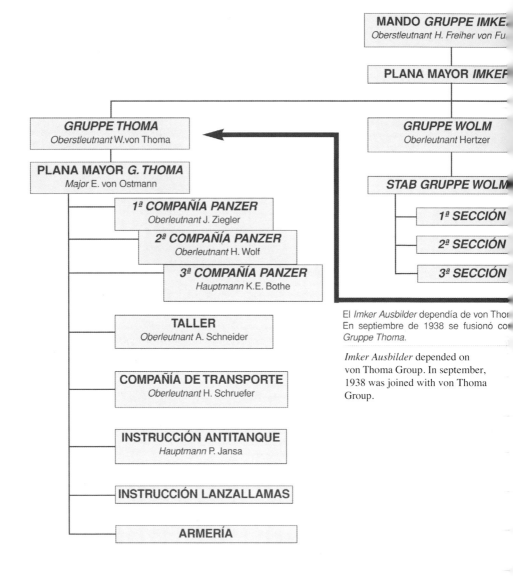

MANDO *GRUPPE IMKE.*
Oberstleutnant H. Freiher von Fu.

PLANA MAYOR *IMKEF*

GRUPPE THOMA
Oberstleutnant W.von Thoma

PLANA MAYOR *G. THOMA*
Major E. von Ostmann

1ª COMPAÑÍA PANZER
Oberleutnant J. Ziegler

2ª COMPAÑÍA PANZER
Oberleutnant H. Wolf

3ª COMPAÑÍA PANZER
Hauptmann K.E. Bothe

TALLER
Oberleutnant A. Schneider

COMPAÑÍA DE TRANSPORTE
Oberleutnant H. Schruefer

INSTRUCCIÓN ANTITANQUE
Hauptmann P. Jansa

INSTRUCCIÓN LANZALLAMAS

ARMERÍA

GRUPPE WOLM
Oberleutnant Hertzer

STAB GRUPPE WOLM

1ª SECCIÓN

2ª SECCIÓN

3ª SECCIÓN

El *Imker Ausbilder* dependía de von Thor
En septiembre de 1938 se fusionó co
Gruppe Thoma.

Imker Ausbilder depended on
von Thoma Group. In september,
1938 was joined with von Thoma
Group.

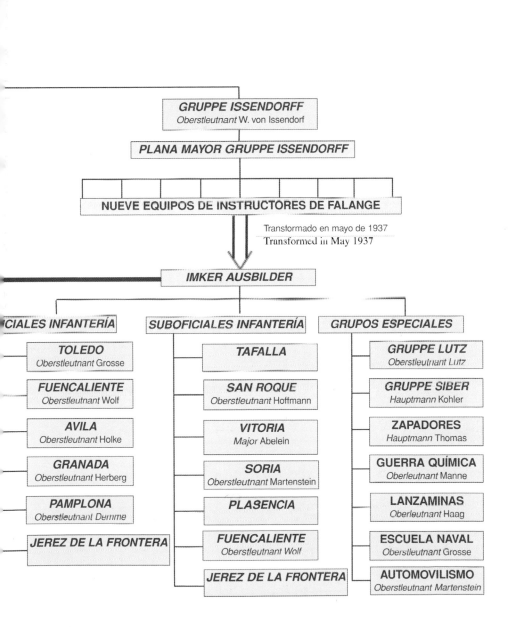

GRUPPE ISSENDORFF
Oberstleutnant W. von Issendorf

PLANA MAYOR GRUPPE ISSENDORFF

NUEVE EQUIPOS DE INSTRUCTORES DE FALANGE

Transformado en mayo de 1937
Transformed in May 1937

IMKER AUSBILDER

CIALES INFANTERÍA

SUBOFICIALES INFANTERÍA

GRUPOS ESPECIALES

TOLEDO
Oberstleutnant Grosse

FUENCALIENTE
Oberstleutnant Wolf

AVILA
Oberstleutnant Holke

GRANADA
Oberstleutnant Herberg

PAMPLONA
Oberstleutnant Demme

JEREZ DE LA FRONTERA

TAFALLA

SAN ROQUE
Oberstleutnant Hoffmann

VITORIA
Major Abelein

SORIA
Oberstleutnant Martenstein

PLASENCIA

FUENCALIENTE
Oberstleutnant Wolf

JEREZ DE LA FRONTERA

GRUPPE LUTZ
Oberstleutnant Lutz

GRUPPE SIBER
Hauptmann Kohler

ZAPADORES
Hauptmann Thomas

GUERRA QUÍMICA
Oberleutnant Manne

LANZAMINAS
Oberleutnant Haag

ESCUELA NAVAL
Oberstleutnant Grosse

AUTOMOVILISMO
Oberstleutnant Martenstein

Appendix 6:
Imker Veterans Awarded *Ritterkreutz* in WWII
(Information supplied by Raúl Arias Ramos & Manuel Álvaro Requena)

HEINRICH BECKER (23-01-1914 /-)
W/O, tank instructor, 08-10-36 to 09-08-37.
RK 15-03-43, *Oberfeldwebel*, 8./Pz.Rgt. 31 (5.Pz-Div.) *Zugführer.*

ALBERT BLAICH (03-10-1913 / 15-03-1945, Hungary)
W/O, *Gruppe Drohne* Staff, 01-10-37 to 31-05-39.
RK 24-07-41, *Oberfeldwebel*, 12./Pz.Rgt. 6 (3.Pz.Div.) *Zugführer.*

ERNST-GEORG BUCHTERKIRCH (10-09-1914 / 17-07-1969)
(*Gruppe Drohne*)
RK 29-6-40, *Oberleutnant*, 2./Pz.Rgt. 6 *Zugführer. Eichenlaub* 31-12-41 *Oberleutnant* 2./Pz.Rgt. 6 commander.

RUDOLF DEMME (03-06-1894 / 05-01-1975, Meckenheim)
Lt Col, Chief Instructor *Academia de Alféreces Provisionales*, Pamplona May 1937 -May 1939.
RK 14-08-1943, *Oberst*, Pz.Gren.Rgt. 59 commander. *Eichenlaub* 28-07-1944, same posting and rank.

OSKAR DIRLEWANGER (26-09-1895, Würzburg / 07-06-1945 Althausen, Württenberg)
1/Lt, Infantry instructor, May-Oct 1937 & Aug 1938-May 1939.
RK 30-09-1944, *Oberführer der Reserve*, SS-Brigade "Dirlewanger" commander.

OSKAR EYSSER (20-12-1911/23-06-1954)
W/O, tank instructor, 08-10-1936 to 20-07-1937.
RK 03-11-1944, *Hauptmann*, 3./Pz.Rgt. 31 (5.Pz.Div.) commander

HANS *FREIHERR* VON FUNCK (23-12-1891, Aachen / 14-02-1979, Viersen, Westfalia)
Lt Col, military attaché at *Cuartel General del Generalísimo* and *Gruppe Imker* responsible since Sept 1936.
RK 15-07-1941 *Generalmajor*, 7.Pz.Div commander. *Eichenlaub*, 22-08-1943 as *Generalleutnant* and same posting.

HELMUT HÖHNO (15-12-1913, Lübbenau, Calau / 17-03-1966, Düsseldorf)
(*Gruppe Drohne*)
RK 09-12-44, Puffendorf, Geilenkirchen *Leutnant*, schw.Pz.Abt. 510 *Zugführer*.

KURT KANNENBERG (08-04-1912, Baltruscheiten, East Prussia / 17-11-44, Puffendorf, Geilenkirchen)
W/O, tank instructor, 08-10-1936 to 30-04-1937. W/O, Nationalist Army Infantry Academy instructor, 01-05-1937 to 31-05-1939).
RK 09-12-1944, *Stabsfeldwebel d. Res.*, 3./schw.Pz.Abt. 506 (9.Pz-Div.) *Zugführer*.

PETER KIESGEN (22-11-1915 /-)
W/O, Infantry instructor, Nov 1938 - May 1939.
RK 05-10-1941, *Leutnant*, 1./IR 23 *Zugführer*.

WOLFGANG VAN KRANENBROCK (11-08-1909, Dresden / 22-03-1986, Erlangen)
2/Lt, Infantry instructor, Nov 1937 to Aug 1938, Section CO.
RK 25-09-42, *Hauptmann*, II./IR 102 commander.

WALTER LUX (24-4-1909, Eydtkuhnen, East Prussia / 10-05-1984, Dachau)
2/Lt, Infantry instructor, Aug 1938 to Apr 1939, Section CO.
RK 10-07-1944, *Major*, GR 316 commander.

KARL PFANNKUCHE (28-09-1909, Dortmund /15-12-1981, Freiburg)
1/Lt, *Gruppe Drohne*, 01-11-1936 to 06-12-1937.
RK 17-03-1945, *Major*, II./Pz.Rgt. 33 (9.Pz.Div.) commander

KARL-HEINZ SORGE (15-04-1914, Lychen, Templin / 23-
10-1963, Evendorp)
W/O, tank instructor, 08-10-36 to 01-07-37.
RK 7-2-44, *Oberleutnant*, 5./Pz.Rgt. 6 (3.Pz.Div.)
commander

WILHELM RITTER VON THOMA (01-09-1991, Dachau
/ 30-04-48, Söcking)
Lt Col, head of the *Gruppe Drohne*, 23-09-1936 to 31-05-1939.
RK 31-12-1941, *Generalmajor*, 20.Pz.Div. commander

WILHELM WENDT (11-10-1911, Friedrischshof, Krs.
Ortelsburg, Ostpreussen / 19-02-1984, Münster)
2/Lt, *Gruppe Drohne* Transport Company, 01-06-1937 to
01-12-1937.
RK 30-06-1941, *Hauptfeldwebel*, 5./Pz.Rgt. 5 *Afrikakorps*

GERHARD WILLING (28-11-1910, Bautzen / 29-10-43,
Krivog Rog, Soviet Union)
Capt, deputy CO of the *2ª Compañia de carros*, 08-10-1936 to 14-09-1937.
RK 07-03-1943, *Major*, III./Pz.Rgt. 33 (9.Pz.Div.) commander

JOACHIM ZIEGLER (18-10-1904, Hanau, Main / 02-05-
1945, Berlin, KIA near Friedrichstrasse r/w station)
     Capt, CO of the *1ª Compañia de carros*, 08-10-1936 1936
01-03-1937. Infantry instructor until 18-03-1938
RK 05-09-44, *SS-Brigadeführer und Generalmajor der Waffen-SS*, 11.SS-
Freiw.Pz.Gren.Div. "Nordland" commander. *Eichenlaub* 28-04-45 (848th
Wehrmacht member so to be awarded) commanding the same unit.

Additional Images

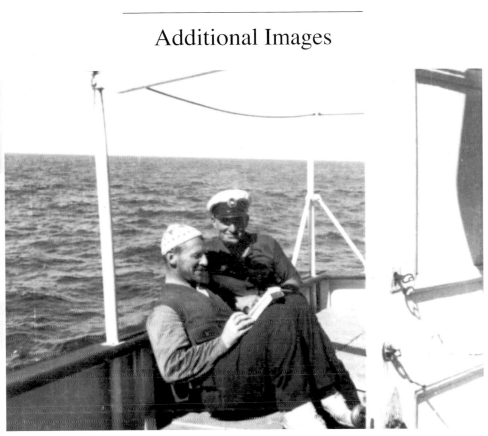

Above: The Captain of the *Girgenti*, Bechstaedt, and supercargo Bücker. (J.M. Campesino, via R. Arias)
Below: The German tank crews wearing civilian clothes, on their trip to Spain on the SS *Girgenti*. (J.M. Campesino, via R. Arias)

Soldiers of Von Thoma

The SS *Girgenti* arriving at her destination, the port of Seville, where men and equipment were landed. (J.M. Campesino, via R. Arias)

Oberstleutnant von Thoma, just arrived to las Herguijuelas Castle, Cáceres, haranguing the first German tank crews that arrived in Spain to establish the armoured unit del Nationalist Army. (J.M. Campesino, via R. Arias)

One de the 37-mm Pak 35/36 anti-tank guns with its tractor, a Krupp L2 Protze. The tank unit had an anti-tank unit armed with eight guns of this model. (J.M. Campesino, via R. Arias)

Standing among several members of the *Gruppe Thoma, comandante* Pujales, CO of the *Batallón de Carros de Combate,* and three captain company COs of the unit. (J.M. Campesino via Raúl Arias)

Several *Panzer I Ausf As* of the Nationalist *Batallón de Carros,* on the main square of a village on a break between operations. (via J, Mazarrasa)

An extraordinary picture of a *Panzerbefehlswagen I Ausf B,* just arrived in Spain. Inside, a Spanish first lieutenant/, flanked by German instructors of the *Drohne.* (via J.M. Mata & F. Marín)

The first operations on the Madrid front by the *Panzer Is* took place in the early days of November 1936. (J.M. Campesino via Raúl Arias)

Two Soviet T-26 B tanks, with clear signs of a hard combat, after their capture by the Nationalists, in a warehouse at Cuatro Vientos. (J.M. Campesino via Raúl Arias)

Two views of the *Panzer I Ausf A* of the *Batallón de Carros* of the Nationalist Army. (via J.M. Mata & F. Marín)

Top, a captured Soviet BA-6 armored car closely inspected by several Nationalist soldiers. Bottom, two Germans of the *Gruppe Thoma* posing by a captured T-26B. (J.M. Campesino via Raúl Arias)

Italian Infantry, standing by the German tanks, ready for the attack on mount Sollube (Bilbao front). (J.M. Campesino via Raúl Arias)

A member of the *Gruppe Thoma* poses for the camera in front of what was left of a destroyed concrete bunker at the Larrabezúa area on 13 June 1937. (J.M. Campesino via Raúl Arias)

The German tanks paraded in different places in Spain after the victory of the Nationalist arms on 1 April 1939. (via Fco. Marín) Below: (via National Library)

Color Gallery

Oberstleutnant Wilhelm *Ritter* von Thoma wearing the overalls he used during the early days in Spain. (October 1936)

2.*Panzerkompanie Gruppe Thoma* sergeant wearing the early uniform, black beret and no badges. (October 1936).

Gruppe Thoma instructor 1st lieutenant wearing the standard *Gruppe* uniform, with the *Panzertruppenabzeichen* badge on the pocket. (March 1937).

Oberstleutnant Wilhelm *Ritter* von Thoma wearing a colonel uniform, black beret and badges. (March 1937).

Panzerkampfwagen 1 Ausf. A

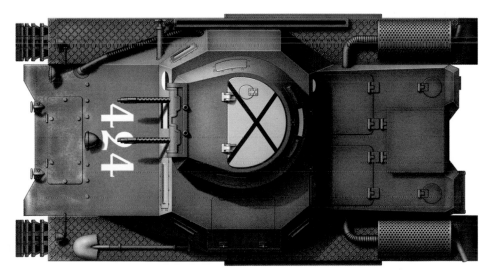

Panzerkampfwagen I Ausf. A, rear view

Panzerbefehlswagen I Ausf. B

Panzerbefehlswagen I Ausf. B, top view

Panzerkampfwagen I Ausf. B

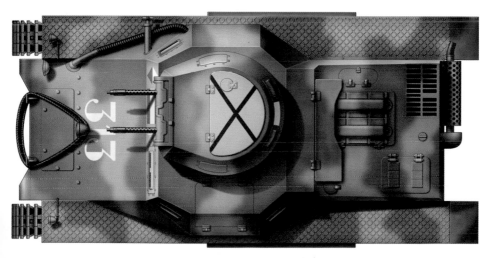

German tank instructor NCO wearing overalls over the *Gruppe Drohne* uniform. (October 1937).

Spanish corporal of the tank battalion wearing overalls and the *Medalla Militar Individual*. (October 1937).

Unteroffizier Hans Joachim Freitag wearing a greatcoat over the *Gruppe* uniform. (March 1937).

Gruppe Thoma emblems and rank badges. A: beret badges. B: *Panzertruppenabzeichen.*
C: rank badges.

German Instructor at the *Academia de Guerra Química* wearing a mustard gas protection suit and German N-24 type mask. (March 1937).

Temporary Infantry second lieutenant wearing a Spanish officer uniform, with a 2nd lieutenant star on black on his chest. (March 1938).

Unteroffizier Alfred Doerschmann, *Escuela Naval Militar* instructor, San Fernando, Cádiz. (May 1938).

Artillery 2nd lieutenant instructor wearing the *Legión Cóndor* uniform, with rank badge on red, Monasterio de Rodilla. (April 1938).

Notes

1 HQs Office for Mobilization, Training and Recovery.
2 Diminutive of *negro*, black in Spanish, a nickname that the Spanish applied to all German personnel and equipment.
3 Major.
4 Russian.
5 Euzkadi tank. Euzkadi is the Basque name for the Basque Country.
6 2nd Lieutenant.
7 *Cía.* is the short for *compañía*.
8 A *tercio* –literally, one third– is about the size of a regiment.
9 A *bandera* –literally, flag– is about the size of a battalion.
10 Group.
11 Disbursing officer.
12 Mobilization, Training and Recovery.
13 All sorts of Nationalist documents of the war years were thus ended with this standard phrase.
14 Corunna's Knights.
15 Automobile Service.
16 The composition of the Falange militias was inspired in the Spanish Foreign Legion and the Italian *fasci di combattimento*. Two *escuadristas* and one *jefe* –chief– made up an *elemento*, three *elementos* and one *jefe* and one *subjefe* –deputy chief– made up an *escuadra* –squadron–. Three *escuadras* (33 men) made up a *falange*. Three *falanges* made up a *centuria*. Three *centurias* made up a *tercio*. Three *tercios* made up a *bandera*. Three *banderas* made up a *legión*.
17 Retired Army *comandante* Pablo Arredondo had established this forerunner of the Falange militias and had started the military training of the organization before the war broke out.
18 Carlist militia.
19 Royal Decree.
20 *Centro Italiano per l'Addestramento di Ufficiali Spagnoli*, Italian School for the Training of Spanish Officers.
21 Marine Corps.
22 Chemical Warfare Manual.
23 In the summer of 1921, around 12,000 Spanish troops were massacred there.
24 Gas Factory.
25 Intelligence Service, Northeast Frontier.
26 Admiral.
27 Lieutenant-Commander.
28 Lieutenant.
29 The Spanish Navy.
30 Illustrious Seamen's Pantheon.

31 A synonimous designation of the Spanish Navy.

32 Artillery Depot.

33 The Irish volunteers.

34 From the German *Blockhaus*.

35 From "tiznado", greyish, the colour they were painted in.

36 S.I.M. stands for *Servicio de Información Militar*, or Military Intelligence Service.

37 *A Thousand Fire Days*. There is no English edition.

38 "*El Novio de la Muerte*", "The Death's Fiancé", the Spanish Foreign Legion's anthem.

39 "The Milkwomen's Donkey", a 1920's popular tune.

40 From a Spanish rhyme, "*El Patio de mi Casa*".

41 A Latin-American popular tune.

Bibliography

Archives
-Archivo General Militar (Ávila)
    Fondos:
    -Cuartel General del Generalísimo (C.G.G.)
    -Zona Nacional (Z.N.)
    -Milicia Nacional. Cuartel General
    -Fondos del Ministerio del Ejército. Libro 42. "Dirección General/ Jefatura de
Movilización, Instrucción y Recuperación (M.I.R.)" boxes 24.607 to 24.681
-Archivo del Ministerio de Asuntos Exteriores (Madrid)
    Fondos:
    -Archivo Renovado
    -Archivo de Burgos
-Archivo de la Zona Marítima del Cantábrico (El Ferrol)

Books
-Alféreces Provisionales. José Mª Gárate Córdoba. Editorial San Martín. Madrid, 1976.
-Blindados en España 1ª parte. Javier de Mazarrasa. Quirón Ediciones. Valladolid
-Carro de combate Verdeja. Javier de Mazarrasa. Carbonell editor. Barcelona, 1988.
-Carros de combate y vehículos blindados de la guerra 1936-1939. F.C. Albert. Borras Ediciones. Barcelona, 1980.
-Das Heer. Uniformes y distintivos. R. Recio y A. González. Arena Editores. Madrid, 1996.
-Die Heeres Nachritentruppe der Wehrmacht, 1935-1945. Hans-Georg Kampe. Podzum-Pallas Verlag, Wpölfersheim-Berstadt, 1994.
-Estampas de la Guerra.
-German light panzers 1932-42. Bryan Perrett. Osprey-Vanguard. London, 1983.
-German Military Intelligence, 1939-1945. Military Inteligence Division, US War Department. University Publications of America. Frederick, Maryland, 1984.
-German Uniforms of the Third Reich 1933-1945. B.L. Davis y P. Turner. Blandford Press. U.K. 1980.
-Historia de las Divisiones del Ejército Nacional 1936-1939. Carlos Engel. Editorial Almena. Madrid, 2000.
-Historia de la Guerra de España. R. Brasillach y M. Bardeche. Valencia, 1966.
-Hitler y la Guerra Civil Española. Misión y destino de la Legión Cóndor. W. von Oven. Editorial Revisión. Argentina 1987
-Intervención extranjera en la Guerra de España. Jesús Salas Larrazábal. Editora Nacional. Madrid, 1974.

-La artillería en la Guerra Civil. Material de origen alemán. Artemio Mortera y José Luis Infiesta. Quirón Ediciones. Valladolid 1994.

-La ayuda alemana a España. R. Hidalgo Salazar. Editorial San Martín. Madrid, 1975.

-La Guerra Civil Española. Hugh Thomas, Ed. Urbión. Madrid, 1987

-La Legión Cóndor

-La Legión Cóndor. España 1936-39. Peter Elstob. Editorial San Martín. Madrid.

-Legión Cóndor. La historia olvidada.L. Molina y J.M. Manrique. Quirón Ediciones. Valladolid, 2000.

-Legion Condor. Uniforms, organization and history. R.J. Bender. R.J. Bender publishing. USA 1992.

-Los carros de combate en España. Javier de Mazarrasa. Editorial San Martín. Madrid, 1977.

-Los carros de combate en la Guerra de España. Javier de Mazarrasa. Quirón Ediciones. Valladolid

-Los catalanes en la Guerra de España. José María Fontana.

-Los datos exactos de la Guerra Civil. Ramón Salas Larrazábal Ediciones Rioduero. Madrid, 1980.

-Los Dossiers secretos de la Guerra Civil. D. Pastor Petit. Editorial Argos. Barcelona, 1978.

-Los otros internacionales. José Luis de Mesa Gutiérrez. Ediciones Barbarroja. Madrid, 1998.

-Los uniformes alemanes de la Segunda Guerra Mundial. P. Marton y G. Verdelago. Editorial De Vecchi. Barcelona, 1981.

-Mil días de fuego. José Mª Gárate Córdoba.

-Nueva y definitiva historia de la Guerra Civil. Ricardo de la Cierva, DINPE. Madrid, 1986.

-Rommel and the secret war in North Africa, 1941-1943. Secret Intelligence in North African Campaign. Janusz Piekalkiewicz. Schiffer Military History, West Chester, Pennsylvania

-Sargentos Provisionales. José Mª Gárate Córdoba. Hermandad Sargentos Provisionales. Madrid, 1977.

-Verbände und Truppen der Deutsche Wehrmacht und Waffen SS. Georg Tessin.

Karl Ries/Hans Ring

THE
LEGION CONDOR
A History of the Luftwaffe
in the Spanish Civil War • 1936-1939

The Legion Condor 1936-1939
Karl Ries Hans Ring

This classic book now makes its first appearance in English. Long out-of-print this study is one of the few books dedicated to the history of the infamous Legion Condor, the German volunteer unit that fought with pro-Franco forces during the Spanish Civil War from 1936-1939. Many of the tactics and strategies of the Luftwaffe were first formulated and used during operations in Spain. Also, various aircraft were tested and used, such as the famous Ju 87, Do 17, He 111 and Bf 109 - all stalwarts of the later Luftwaffe during World War II. Many Luftwaffe pilots received combat training in Spain; Werner Molders and Adolf Galland first earned their wings as members of the Legion Condor. Renowned Luftwaffe experts Karl Ries and Hans Ring have brought together over 480 photographs, including aerial reconnaissance photos, detailed unit insignia, and action shots. The history of the Legion Condor is discussed in great detail, including the many personalities, thorough battle analysis, and technical aspects of the weaponry. The result is a superb historical study of the early Luftwaffe. Karl Ries is the author of many books on the Luftwaffe including Luftwaffe Rudder Markings 1936-1945 with Ernst Obermaier, available from Schiffer Military History. Hans Ring is co-author with Werner Girbig of a unit history of JG 27.

ISBN: 0887403395 8 1/2" x 11"   288 pp   hard cover $49.95

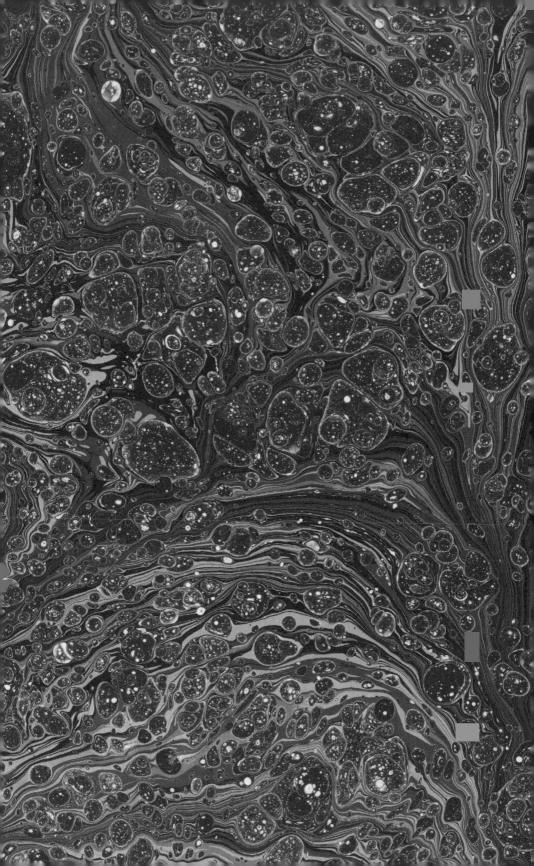